Conte

.

Acknowledgements and Introduction

In the name of the most merciful and compassionate, I begin this book with endless and genuine gratitude for his blessings on everyone and everything in his ever-expanding universe that includes me. My sincere gratitude also goes to everyone who made this book possible to see the light, and I really mean everyone, from the people who encouraged and challenged me to write my own book in my own words, to the people who made this book legible and available for you to read including Elisabeth Galvin. Another appreciation to my mentors, Mohamed Ali, Randah Taher, and Kat Fernandes. Special gratitude goes to you, as you have decided to invest your precious time, energy, and money to read my book. Without unnecessary reference to scientific backup, I can vouch from experience that the emotion of gratitude is the most powerful and precious feeling that we all could ever possess and extend to one and other. My gratitude is the best gift I received in my life and I want to extend it in abundance to every one of you.

Not only the thought of writing my own book was a fanciful and intimidating thought for me, not to mention the lack of experience and English fluency but I was also terrified and hesitant in putting my life out there in public, both literally and metaphorically. The notion of fostering inspirations and sharing meaningful ideas is what has propelled me to overcome this hesitation. Therefore, and while the details of this book are based on the story of my life, its purpose is certainly much bigger than myself. Connecting with my life purpose and the intention to extend my gratitude to my mother (Ambera) is what has truly inspired me to embark on this mission. Additionally, while I have attempted to obtain the permission of everyone to include their names in this book, I want to apologize profusely to anyone who I might have caused him/her discomfort in any shape or form; either through the content of this book or generally through my words and actions during our interactions. After all, this book is going to be one of my legacies in this universe; I pray to His Mighty to accept anything good that might come out of it and to forgive me for any ill-informed thoughts I might have unwittingly contemplated or shared in this book or in any other moment of my existence.

While I have no idea about how this book is going to be received, I am sharing with you the commitment that I made to God that I'll donate a minimum of 20 per cent of the proceedings of this book to fulfill humanitarian initiatives that I want to launch in memory of my mum who passed away in 2016. These initiatives will include building a decent and more secure house for my family and sponsoring the education cost of children including my nephews and nieces in Somalia. I believe charity starts at home and I am planning that I later expand these initiatives to wider communities. I am also vouching I'll operate these initiatives in the most transparent and fair possible way. My mum gave her blood, sweat, and tears to secure my education, so extending this gift to others, is the best way to honor her legacy. No matter what I do or say, I'll never feel that I could thank her sufficiently for all the love and sacrifices that she extended to me, my father my siblings, to her community and relatives, or to anyone else in this world who she touched in some aspects of their lives.

Additionally, and while I did my best to stay truthful to my own values in this life that I shared through social and theological lenses in this book, I want to invite you all to properly reflect on what has resonated with you or otherwise. Ponder on all that you read in this book, both literally or what you digest between the lines and make an informed decision in your own life. In other words, I am inviting you to feel deeply and think critically while enjoying every precious moment that you are spending before, during, and after the time you have kindly designated to read this book. You might decide to take everything I say with a pinch of salt, laugh with hysteria, cry passionately, pick insights that are relevant to you, or simply enjoy the triumphs and tribulations of my journey. Frankly, the choice is yours.

I only hope that I'll do justice to what your heart, mind, and soul are ultimately longing for.

Every heart is made of a unique story and I will be fulfilled and delighted if the content of this book manages to ignite a spark of inspiration within you; I hope you begin to feel that you are larger than the space that you are currently occupying and be able to be more inquisitive to learn from the universe, by living in a regular and steady state of expansion.

In this spirit of expansion through learning, I am attempting to share with you through the art of storytelling, some of my most precious values in life. These values include gratitude, authenticity, justice, equity, inclusion, independence, resilience, perseverance, excellence, and adventure.

For me, upholding these values is only possible as a result of divine connection. While there are many ways to live with these values, I learned from my mother and through life experience that the gifts of intention, intuition, and reflection are what is required to live a fulfilling and purposeful life.

Chapter 1

The Routes

My life began before I came into the world. When my mum was pregnant, my nine-year-old brother, Ismail, was killed by a car on his way back from school.

Oblivious to the accident, Mum was deep in prayer as her friends rushed to her to share the tragic news. She would not be interrupted; when she finished her dedications and heard Ismail was critically ill in hospital, she was overcome by an aura of complete calm. Out of a total belief in Allah's will, she carefully dusted herself down and made her way to the hospital. When she arrived too late, she gently repeated, "Enna leallah, wenna ellihi rajeoon"—"We are the Lord's creation and we shall return to him."

My birth, then, was much anticipated, as Mum and everyone who knew our family prayed to God that he would deliver another baby to comfort the loss of Ismail. When I came into the world some months later, everyone rejoiced, and I was given seven different names meaning "the replacement" and "the new joy".

Our home was a small town called Holwathek in Mogadishu, in Somalia. My dad was in the army and my mum was self-employed as a butcher.

We were eight siblings of four boys and four girls and I am the youngest of the boys. Unfortunately, Ismail was the second sibling that we lost. My second-oldest sister Nestaiho, passed away at a young age from a mysterious illness, a few years before his death.

Unlike a lot of marriages back in Somalia, my dad and mum were not related. But due to the incompatibility of their genes, three of their children were born blind including me. I don't write this with irony when I say that I am grateful to God for the gift of my sight-loss. I was born with retinal dystrophy, which means I have very limited vision during the day and virtually nothing, at night. The doctors tell me that during the daytime I have about 20 per cent vision: at night, it is barely 2 per cent. During the brightest possible daylight, I can be confident enough to cycle a bike. But I might misjudge how close someone is to me. At night, I wouldn't even consider putting one foot in front of the other for fear of falling over something. Another way to describe what I can and can't see is that if someone is directly under the sun, that is the clearest possible way for me to see them. But at night, I can't tell if a person is there or not. I use touch when I want to verify something but I don't usually touch people's faces. I do my best to look at them in the best possible light— literally and figuratively! I now use a white stick, but as a child, I would memorise routes so I could walk around.

My memory of my childhood in Somalia is vague and blurry, yet I can recall some moments that I fondly cherish. I remember that our home was situated in the heart of Mogadishu and our house was very small and made of corrugated-tin with small ventilations to keep us cool all year round. We had no electricity or running water although, thank God, that our climate is mild and pleasant all year round. As is typical in Somalia, we had cats, dogs, chickens, roosters, and goats.

As Muslims, our family adhered to a clear daily schedule with all its rituals. Each day started with waking up at dawn to pray, the first of five for every one of puberty age and above. Being young, I was not required to pray but I was eager to learn and participate. I remember hanging around afterward to observe magnificent sunrises as birds sungaway.

Inside, Mum would be busy simultaneously preparing the breakfast while preparing her sharp knife for a rather arduous task.

Each day she brought the goats out of their cage and would wrestle them to the ground, one goat at a time.

I still remember the sound as she sharpened her knife and just as the goat looked away for a split second, she slaughtered the animal from the neck, whilst saying, "In the name of Allah, the compassionate and merciful God."

Mum then swiftly skinned and cut the goat into small pieces, just as easily as you would cut your salad. It scared the hell out of me the first time I saw this butchering scene, but I soon got used to the daily drill.

Elsewhere, my father would get ready to go to his military job as my siblings and I rushed around to get to school. My oldest blind brother was a teacher at Dukssi, the local Quran school I attended. All Somalis, no matter their background, will ensure their children join their local Dukssi to memorise the Quran. It's the ultimate pride for a family. My school was simple, and I learnt the Arabic script of the Quaran from a wooden board which I learnt by rote repetition with the rest of the class (there was no writing or reading just memorizing). No one was ever late for school. All these years later, I realize that the commitment to education by Somali children and their families instilled in us all great discipline and a strong Muslim identity.

I have been adventurous and mischievous all my life. My earliest memories are of roaming the alleyways in search of adventure including my favourite game of sitting under our neighbor's tree and throwing stones upwards to catch the fruit. Of course, I ended up with plenty of leaves and a cut head with blood streaming down my chest and back. As soon as the wounds healed, I'd be back under that tree again.

I've always been curious and would bore everyone with my endless questions. My other favourite activity, especially in the morning before school, would be to go to our local grocery shop to observe how the owner sells his wares. It was more the assistant of the shop I was interested in: a monkey. Well-trained, it could fetch money from customers and bring their required items to the counter. It was my ambition to be that monkey's assistant, and I was duly employed as such. It was my first job and inspired an entrepreneurial spirit in me that I've never lost.

Such zest for life has made me trusting of most people I meet; Mum would never worry when I didn't come back for dinner as I'd be sleeping over in a different neighbor's house each night. Apparently, I'd come home to give the family a full report about what I'd been doing and who I was with.

I escaped a major tragedy as a child. Two of my siblings hadn't survived childhood and I nearly didn't either. I was with my friend Sadeq, crossing the road toward the market. There are very few pedestrian crossings in Somalia and we had to cross at our own risk. A white van approached us on our left-hand side: we thought the driver was slowing down to allow us to cross but instead, he sped up. I ran across the road as fast as I could to avoid him, however, I was hit by the car but only on the edge, which in fact knocked me closer to the safety of the pavement with only minor bruises. But Sadeq was a step behind me and died.

The incident changed our family. Flashbacks to Ismail's death meant that my parents became much stricter and I was more or less confined to the house except to go to school until I was offered an unexpected escape route.

God made everything possible for Mum to empower me to receive a very special education when I was seven years old.

She heard of a scholarship to study in a private school for the visually impaired in Bahrain, in the Middle East. My parents could not miss this opportunity and I was put forward for an assessment. I passed the test, but wasn't selected. That was until an unexpected place became available after two current students were not allowed to return to the school on the grounds of mental health.

I was in! Mum was overjoyed but, at the same time, concerned about how to pay for my flight to Bahrain. Throughout my life, I have found that desperate times unleash creative solutions to solve a problem and this was true for Mum: she learned a new skill to make her butchering business more profitable. By processing goat skin into fine leather and accepting offers of loans from neighbors, she made enough money for my airline ticket.

As Mum said goodbye and handed me my bag, I can still remember that she packed me a packet of biscuits and the Somali sweet halwa. I can still remember the taste of it.

Dad drove me to the airport where I met my friend and fellow student, Osman, standing there in his white trousers and a blue jacket with white stripes on the arms. I could just about make him out in the bright sun.

Osman was a comfort to me. We expected my dad and his uncle to come with us on the flight but as we checked in, they told us the plane was just for children. They promised they would fly over a few days later.

As the plane took off, Osman and I exchanged our silly and innocent children's jokes, inventing our own vocabulary. It would later become our own unique way of communication in the unknown world of our new home, the Al Noor School.

We knew our lives were about the change, but we expected to be home again after a few months of learning Arabic.

Chapter 2
Sink or Swim

We landed in Bahrain in October 1990. At the time, the Al Noor was the best private school for blind people in the Middle East and extremely well-funded by the Arab Gulf countries, attracting students from across the Arab world. It had everything you could imagine in terms of facilities from a mosque to a sports complex complete with a swimming pool, a huge theater hall, and a garden with an abundance of flowering fruit trees. The staff was enormous, from catering, security, cleaners, drivers, runners, and laundry services. As blind students, we had every materialistic thing provided to us on a plate.

The school was divided into halves, one for teenage boys and young men and the other half, for younger children and females. Classes were taken downstairs with just nine students in each. Upstairs was the accommodation; each room would host three of us.

We were taught a full curriculum entirely in Braille including Arabic and English languages to science, math, sports, music, and art. For students with learning difficulties, there were vocational classes such as handcrafting for boys and knitting for girls. Type-writing classes were available from Year 7.

Being plunged into that environment from our home in Somalia was a shock. I spoke not a word of Arabic and I was expecting my father to arrive after three days. I woke up so excited in anticipation of his arrival. I was bitterly disappointed when I realized he didn't mean it.

It was difficult for me to comprehend what I was going through. I remember gazing with my limited vision through the window before being approached by a girl wearing glasses and She-esmek?"—"What is your name?" I didn't understand what she was asking and felt fragile. Tears soon appeared and I ran out of the classroom crying, throwing myself on the ground of the school's middle podium. I lay there crying, wanting to be with my family rather than strange people like the girl in glasses. It was a defining moment for me, and I felt every painful part of separation anxiety. I felt like a fish taken out of water.

The thing was, I would have been able to go home in six months' time for the summer holidays. Except that the Iraq invasion of Kuwait that year of 1990 meant it was not possible to leave Bahrain. We were often told to remain indoors to avoid the risk of being hit by a missile.

Even if it had been possible to fly out of the Middle East, something much, much worse had happened at home without my knowing it. The terrible civil war in Somalia had broken out. The overthrow of the military regime of President Siad Barre, the year after I started at Al Noor, tore the country apart.

I knew nothing of this especially as Osman and I were the only Somali boys in the children and female accommodation. There was one other Somali girl but, otherwise, everyone else was Arab.

Being away from my family in this strange environment was beginning to have a physiological as well as psychological effect on me. Each morning when I woke up, I would have wet the bed. The shame was worsened when the female warden who woke us up for dawn prayers would shout at us for being "dirty boys", slap our faces, hit us with her slipper, and then, beat us with a wooden clothes hanger all across our bodies. She would drag us by the ear or arm to the shower room, strip us naked, and shove us under the cold shower. We were then forcefully dressed with threats of worse punishment should we do it again.

It happened every day because of course we would go to bed frightened of the punishment and wet the bed again.

What was worse was the taunts by the other children who made fun of my misery, bullying me for what was happening. Meanwhile, the wardens were rewarded and praised for helping to 'cure' those 'naughty and dirty boys'.

Chapter 3
What Doesn't Kill you, Makes you Stronger

A l Noor was managed by what I felt was an old-school autocrat. Well-connected and trusted by highly influential figures in Bahrain, she was able to secure a huge amount of funding for the school. She intimidated everyone from her deputy to the lowest-ranking employee. But she was a strange mixture: there was a peculiar touch of compassion in her personality, which I was to find myself at the receiving end of.

One day in grade three, I left a boring lesson to go into the bathroom. I decided to spill water all over myself, jumping up and down in total joy and screaming in amusement. After the thrill of the shower faded, I went to the sink, grabbed the metal plug, and started to hammer the edges of the sink. I kept hammering, and, to the delight of my childishness, managed to break one side of the sink. At this point, the principal walked in and slapped me across the face while shouting abuse at me. I can still hear the echo of that slap in the bathroom. Yet during the weeks that followed, whenever she saw me as she drove in and out of school, she would call me over affectionately to check my bruised head.

She was a powerful woman and had her grip on everything to do with the school, from the most trivial matter to vital affairs. We saw quite how powerful she was when she expelled a rebellious student on the spot in front of the whole school after he answered her back. Within less than 14 hours he was on a plane to Oman with no return.

With (what we felt) a dictator at the helm, we had a very strict schedule at Al Noor, from food to lessons. No student no matter what their age was ever allowed to leave the building unless they underwent rigorous paperwork. Very few visitors were allowed. There was 24-hour security. The best way to describe Al Noor, at that time, was a five-star maximum-security prison.

We had no control nor choice of anything in our lives. Well, perhaps we had control of our breath, or at least, when we were not tortured. We had no choice of what to eat or choice of which activities we participated in. Everything we said and did was monitored by wardens and followed by a daily written report to the management.

Our entire day was well-rehearsed, from the moment we woke up at dawn until our room curfew of 8 pm.

As Somali students, we received 10 BHD – equivalent to 25 USD per month as allowance. We would be allowed to spend 50 cents each day. Per month, that meant we spent 15 USD with the remaining 10 USD kept as savings. We, as Somali students, felt it was suffocating because our Gulf Arab peers were allowed to spend lavishly from their government-sponsored budget. Whenever we wanted to withdraw any small amount of money, we had to go to the finance admin at the school to make a case of why we needed the money. We had to have our fingerprints taken before the bank would authorize the request. The school had a power of attorney to conduct all our financial affairs on our behalf, without our consent or knowledge.

The curriculum would hardly ever be updated. The school's facilities and small classes of nine students were excellent but the caliber of teachers varied from very poor to outstanding, a significant factor that made me poor in math and excel at geography. The majority of non-teacher staff were unqualified and uneducated with harsh attitudes and no understanding of the needs of blind people. Verbal and physical abuse as well as public humiliation was a daily drill.

Chapter 4

A Light at the End of the Tunnel

In the middle of all this horrendous experience, God was helping me cope. I had to learn Arabic to survive and was pleased to receive an award for the fastest non-Arab student to learn Arabic. In fact, to the astonishment of everyone including myself, my academic results would consistently be amongst the highest in the school.

I managed to squeeze in the odd moment of pleasure such as becoming addicted to the Arabic football cartoon, Captain Majid, and obsessively collecting as many picture cards as I could of the character. I spent my breakfast money on small packets of biscuits containing character cards in the hope of collecting a new one for my album.

But even the simple joy of watching a children's cartoon was made difficult. I couldn't afford a watch so never knew what the time was but I worked out when the cartoon was on at 10. 10am by following the school building's shadow. At weekends, when it would hit the drainage, I knew my cartoon would be on so I'd run to the common room to watch it.

Back home in Somalia, the civil war was taking its toll and sadly claiming thousands of lives. In the middle of the chaos, I lost any contact with my family and heard nothing from them for four years. My fear and anxiety about my family made things unbearable. I began to give up hope of ever going back there and slowly forgot my Somali language as I spoke Arabic every day.

But in 1994, God's blessing found a way of reuniting us. My family managed to contact me after placing several adverts in the local media and through the BBC. Once my family found the details of my school, they were able to resume contact and sent me recorded messages on cassette tapes.

By then, my Somali was too shabby for me to communicate back to them. Thank God my older friend, Abdullah Dershe, translated what my family was saying to me and sent my message back to them. I owe Abdullah a huge gratitude for this and the other ways he helped me at Al Noor.

When reflecting on it now, the cassettes were a rather strange and primitive method of communication compared to today's instant messages. It would take around three months for the cassette to arrive and a similar length of time to return back. When the tape arrived, all of us Somali students would gather in numbers around the recorder, listening for 90 minutes digesting and reflecting on every word. Osman, the friend who came with me on the plane to Al Noor, hadn't heard from his family. We would keep rewinding and forwarding back and forth to make sure that we have not missed anything. The tape would always begin with my oldest blind brother. He is well-versed in religious studies, which gave him a highly respected status in the family and society. Saad would then invite my parents, siblings, and all the neighbors to take a turn in recording their regards and messages to me. The background noise was always lively with children playing and adults engaging in lively debates. Reflecting on this experience makes me nostalgic.

After exchanging a couple of tapes, I could not hide from Mum the tortures that I was being subjected to by the wardens. I told her everything, knowing that she had always been there for me.

Even though she was thousands of miles away and physically powerless to protect me, Mum was well-known and highly respected amongst our tribe. She contacted relatives who work as traders in Dubai and informed them what was going on at Al Noor. Those relatives then contacted the management at the school, denouncing their barbaric treatment towards me. This sent a message to the management that there were people outside of the school who would do whatever it took to defend me. Even though this protest didn't directly translate to a change in the way I was treated, it made me so proud of Mum's endeavors to minimize my suffering.

A very surprising development in 1995 changed everything at Al Noor when the school board ousted the principal. She refused to leave and divided the staff into those who supported her and those who didn't. As students, we were forced to swear with our fingerprints we would support the newly appointed principal. On the same day in the evening, we were coerced by the wardens to sign the same documents showing our allegiance to the ousted principal.

As students, we decided to amuse ourselves by marching in small demonstrations against the ousted principle while enjoying all sorts of gossip. We had plenty of free time to gather in the common room exchanging the latest school dramatic news, before moving to heated debates about politics, religion, and even sex (oh yes, blind people talk about sex too!).

You can just imagine the exuberant atmosphere of dozens of blind people shouting as loud as possible to put their point across, making up for missing visual cues. Whenever we got bored of debating, we would continue arguing and laughing while playing the Braille versions of Dominos, Uno, and chess.

Outside the common room, the school's entrenched political battlefield was causing huge uncertainty and creating an intimidating and toxic atmosphere. The stalemate carried on for months with the ousted principle refusing to leave her office despite much diminished influence while the newly appointed principal timidly tried to exert his influence. Finally, the police security denied the ousted principal access to the premises, ushering her away, at last. She never returned and no one ever knew where she went.

Chapter 5

Every Patience Pays Off

As I neared puberty I was transferred to the adults' accommodation. At the same time, the new principal (a teacher) was trying to improve the pastoral care of the school. He appointed a daytime warden who was tasked with investigating my problem of wetting the bed during sleep. After five years of relentless psychological and physical torture, I was for the first time being treated like a human being. After being medically examined by the hospital, the doctor recommended that I was transferred to a psychological unit as there was no physical reason for my condition. After a few counselling sessions, the psychiatrist insisted that I was placed each night in a unit for traumatized young people. It meant I only had to go to Al Noor in the morning for lessons but would live in the unit for the rest of the time.

It is an understatement to say that this change in circumstances was a defining moment in my life; I will be forever grateful to God. I was finally being protected from daily psychological and physical abuse and offered care rather than being criminalized. It was liberating to be away from the abusive and harsh environment of Al Noor. I was not the only one to find comfort in the unit and I began to regain both the innocence and dignity that I had been deprived of for many years.

I started to enjoy playing with other children, interacting without any bullying or blame for wetting the bed. It was a complete rehabilitation program that lasted for several months. I underwent regular counseling as well as physical care to overcome the bed wetting: this combination of care and a feeling of safety was sufficient to cure what was proven to be a deeply-rooted anxiety complication.

After that dark episode was over, I started to enjoy life and regained my confidence and the swagger that characterized my childhood in Somalia. Around 15 years old, I found myself attracted to a girl who in turn had a crush on my friend and, ironically, her friend had a big crush on me. We were all running in a circle of teenage lust whereby someone is interested in someone else without the other person reciprocating. We would do outlandish things to get each other's attention. The girls would give us gifts and throw everything at us. I, on the other hand, did something outlandish during a school trip to the funfair.

As we boarded one of the roller coasters, my would-be love interest challenged me to unfasten my belt and stand up while hanging in the air. In a split second, I stood up with both hands raised in celebration. The staff were so shocked with my moment of madness they immediately disabled the roller-coaster and made an announcement on the microphone urging me to return to my seat.

A few days later, I wrote a love letter to her and placed it in her classroom's table-drawer. When she found the letter the next day, the girl reported me to the principal out of ego to show everyone I was in love with her. I received a verbal warning from the principal which I forgot as soon as I left his office.

While the principal was an improvement, the newly appointed warden was a mixed blessing. He left the darkest psychological scars on my memory. As well as the warden, this man was the Imam (prayer-leader) in our local mosque and one of the nicest people you could ever meet, always helping anyone in need with impeccable manners. Yet, he turned out to be the most untrustworthy person. Students began reporting that their money was going missing including an orphan who found all his shopping money had disappeared, on the eve of his return to his native country. He was distressed because it meant he would return empty-handed to his family with no gifts to offer.

The incidents of money theft kept happening at an alarming rate, from the largest amounts to the most trivial amount. While we all had bad habits, the students were adamant that none of us would be cowardly enough to steal money from each other. This led to the unthinkable conviction: it was the warden who was the thief. I and a friend, Ibrahim, decided to put the confusion to bed at last.

One evening, as all students were in the dining-room, we left 10 BHD on the table in Ibrahim's room. The warden was carrying out his duty of distributing clean school uniforms in the wardrobe of each student. After he left Ibrahim's room, we noticed the money was no longer there. The Ishaa (the last prayer), was our chance. As the warden was about to read us the regular religious citation, I rudely interrupted him. The entire mosque became very tense with an explosive atmosphere. While none of us as blind students could see the face of the warden, at that particular moment, we knew what he was thinking. It was an embarrassing moment for him and he responded with uncontrollable anger, protesting his innocence. He reached the lowest point of his credibility by physically assaulting me, and pushing me back against the window. All my fellow students rushed to separate us. After the incident, the warden suddenly became extremely friendly and generous towards Ibrahim. The warden never stole again, and I subsequently led a campaign with other students to have locks fitted on our cupboards.

Chapter 6

The Dichotomy of Risk and Trust

My best memory of Al Noor comes from sport. The school employed a wonderful full-time PE teacher called Abdallah Alnajem; a teacher who came with so much enthusiasm to make a significant impact, which he did without question. He challenged the management to open the swimming pool that had been closed since it was built. His efforts sadly came to nothing when a bizarre circumstance caused a blind student with an intellectual disability to almost drown on the same day the pool opened. The student survived but the pool was closed again.

Yet Abdallah was not to be swayed from transforming the school's recreational and sport activities. He managed to completely revamp the gym and the outdoor recreational facilities, built a new 5-side football pitch and organized tournaments.

He challenged the notion that blind people cannot enjoy the sport of cycling and made the cycling center safe for us by fitting ramps and a fence. We were trained on single bikes and also tandems, where a partially-blind student rides with a totally blind student. My best friend, Osman, was the master of using echoing techniques to allow blind students to ride a single bike independently: he would make a noise with his tongue and the echo of this noise would rebound from the fences back to his ears enabling him to locate his position and be in control of his speed. Abdallah even organized a formal competition for cycling, which was so much fun.

When reflecting on what Abdallah achieved, I learn that any creativity or transformation (either on a personal or organizational level), requires a delicate balance between flexibility and perseverance. I realize that for any risk in life (no matter how small), it needs to be complemented with trust. A clear vision to keep focused on the mission is essential to overcome challenges on the way. It helps to develop a thick skin in the face of criticisms and failure as Abdallah had all those skills in abundance even though he was not a graduate of management school. Abdallah was just determined and creative in a vision and was willing to put so much effort into it.

The final change in staff came with a new warden from Egypt. I was bitterly disappointed when I heard the news, as I had suffered all my past tortures in the hands of Egyptian wardens. But when Mohamed-Salih finally arrived on 7 April 1999, I was pleasantly surprised by his character and pedigree. He was well-educated unlike his Egyptian predecessors, had experience in working with disabled students and, above all, was a very honest and decent gentleman.

It took a few months until he won over our fragile trust. Not only he was respectable and transparent in his inter-actions, but he had (to our astonishment) our interests at heart above the agenda of the management that employed him. Under his supervision, we were finally allowed to enjoy a normal youth lifestyle. We had a lot more freedom because he treated us like his younger brothers—sharing with us plenty of adventures and jokes.

In addition, we owe him further gratitude because as I entered secondary school, I had to study in a mainstream school without sufficient support. This meant that my academic results had plummeted. As a blind student, I had been enrolled in a school with no appropriate tran-sitional training—for me or the teachers. I wasn't given a white stick, nor offered support to read the teachers' instructions on the whiteboard. No accessible books nor suitable devices to take any notes were provided. We just had to rely on our memory to sit exams and hope for the best. However, Mohamed-Salih was kind enough to help us revise all our subjects and got us through the exams—just.

After persevering in this mainstream school for a couple of years, I felt that my life in Bahrain could not be sustainable. As I got wiser in age and experience, I became aware of the reality of the ex-pats living in the Middle East. I was living on a renewable residency visa with no right to permanent residency or citizenship or access to free higher education. I realized my future was becoming increasingly bleak. I had to seriously consider what options I had for a more secure and dignified future. Speaking with my older Somali peers, some had successfully migrated to the UK, and a few of them had returned to Somalia after they had been provided with empty promises of better education. The rest tried their luck in Syria and Egypt.

Once again, when I felt my back against the wall I reached out to God in my prayers—praying for his blessings, in which I was certain of its abundance. I started to contact almost every relative of mine who lived abroad in an attempt to secure my next move. Everything that I hoped for started to diminish over time. In a moment of desperation, I called my mum, sharing my concerns for the future. It must have been so hard for her, knowing we would be separated for longer. But once again, her composure was truly remarkable as she said: "God will have the ultimate will in this, and in his will we trust."

That response gave me a total sense of serendipity and filled my heart and mind with peace. I have always remembered her wisdom because as humans, we are primarily in charge of our intention and endeavors.

Outcomes might correspond or contradict the process of our intentions and endeavors, but there are always unknown benefits in the outcomes which are orchestrated with foresight by the one who produces all results. This is not to undermine the role of science or logic, but to seek comfort in submitting to the will of God while exploring every avenue with effort.

Ultimately, Al Noor's impact was a source of strength. I learned the world out there is tough and I had to stand up for myself: it developed in me a way to cope with adversity, and unless I had gone through the rough of life, I will never have a character to build. I'm grateful to God that I didn't become depressed. It made me even more determined to make the most out of my life and make up for every moment I lost.

Within 48 hours of that phonecall, I was informed that there was an invitation for me to come to the UK via fax. It had come from an uncle of mine in the UK who happened to be an ophthalmologist. Dr Dallmar had been the one who facilitated my scholarship to Bahrain, in 1990. Once again, he was to change the course of my life.

Everything happened so fast and I barely had time to say goodbye to my friends and Al Noor. A few days from when I heard the news, Osman and I were, once again, by ourselves on a plane embarking on our next adventure. A risky but necessary adventure in the search of a brighter future, as a return to Somalia, remained a life-threatening risk.

Chapter 7
Unlimited Horizons

I had all sorts of perceptions about the UK being a futuristic world of fiction where everything is advanced and flawless.

When I arrived, I was shocked to see homelessness, lack of safety, violence, and substance addiction. I was surprised to see that people drove on the same types of roads as in the Middle East but lived in very old houses and followed traditions. I had imaged something much more sci-fi!

My friend, Abdallah Dirshe, the Somali from Al Noor, picked us up from the airport and welcomed us with open arms to his house. He had been in the same position as us, some five years before, but had already settled well into UK life with his unique style of communication, incredible sense of humor, huge network, and general knowledge of multiple societal and political affairs.

He helped us to embrace our new reality as we were put up in turns by old friends from Al Noor and received a wake-up call to face the reality of a world outside school. I will always remember the first time I tried to make breakfast for myself at age 18. After buying some bread and eggs from the local grocery store, I cracked the egg on the kitchen table in anticipation to peel the shell off and eat it with the bread. To my genuine astonishment, I could not understand why the egg was not solid from the inside, but instead was sticky and watery. I rang Ahmed— one of our Alnoor friends in London saying, "I've heard of the cow disease in the UK, but what is the matter with the eggs in this country"? He laughed hysterically and opened my blind eyes to living life on my own. As I had never been in a kitchen previously, believe it or not, I basically did not realize the egg must be boiled before the inside becomes a solid and edible shape.

As much as the egg incident is a funny moment, it was also a time when I received the most precious gift life has given me, something that I will cherish for the rest of my existence: independence. Al Noor's excessive protection had impaired my potential and prevented me from the gift that some will never be offered.

This realization has ever since encouraged me to fully embrace the gift of independence. I swiftly learned vital life skills including cooking, cleaning, and DIY, as well as being able to move and travel independently outside the house. The local social services team visited and introduced me to a new world of domestic and mobility autonomy as I learned to utilize all my other senses to make up for my lack of vision. For the first time, I used a white cane for independent mobility. I still remember my social worker telling me that my academic ambitions had no meaning without essential life skills. Life felt so different after I'd made my first meal (Somali spaghetti-Bolognese) and made my first trip on the local train between Wembley and Kilburn, in north-west London.

This new lifestyle not only meant more independence but it also built on my ability to withstand the unfamiliar territory of physical deprivation and hardship. As my savings dried up, I found myself not able to afford to eat more than one hot meal a day, and as the situation got worse, I had to go several days living only on dry cornflakes and tap water. I knew my friends would have been glad to help me during this tough financial situation and even been upset with me for not letting them know what I was going through. But I made this choice to learn how to better manage my finances and, more importantly, to preserve my dignity as I was confident that God would ease my situation while I was waiting for income. It was the case. I received my first unemployed government assistance payment.

After a year of life-skills rehabilitation, I enrolled at Westminster College. At first, I just wanted to enroll in

English classes but I was encouraged to join IT classes for the visually impaired. It was Andy, the disability coordinator, and Lucy, the IT teacher, who took the time to explain how I would benefit from these additional classes. They would become my informal mentors and two people who made a big difference in my life. I wasn't sure at first: I had never touched a computer before and was afraid of my limited English communication.

My encounter in that class was another example of the sink or swim type of experience I was faced with: I could either have my self-esteem shattered or I could build the next arsenal of confidence and resilience. Thanks be to God that the former was the case. Lucy did everything she could to facilitate my inclusion and learning, despite the criticisms directed at me by her assistant. This person seemed unwilling to accept me in the class and often criticized me with sarcasm for the smallest mistake I made. But I was not willing to accept her attempt to shackle my potential and I passed the required assessments in both English and IT skills.

The experience increased my appetite for a more profound challenge and I enrolled in a boarding college outside London to complete a comprehensive vocational course. There were two motivations for doing this. While I was speared by my positive experience at Westminster, I was also motivated by a negative experience within my social circle. While I was grateful for the care and support of my ethnic community for easing my transition into the UK, I had become resentful of the limitations people in that community placed on themselves. They wanted me to adopt the same mindset of keeping the minimum ambition target. When I told them about my ambition of completing university and landing a decent job, some of them would laugh at me.

"Yahye, don't kid yourself. You are blind and black. Who is going to employ you?"

This vicious circle of negativity threatened to creep into my thoughts and emotions. I empathized with the causes of their resentfulness which was rooted in deep societal inequality. Of course, their passive and most likely unconscious decision to accept this inequality had certainly perpetuated this vicious cycle of inequality.

It was summer and there was nothing else to keep me occupied, so I found myself indulging with them in endless debates over extended meals and tea sessions. Later, I would regularly join them for long nights of qat, a popular type of drug in Somalia. After a couple of months I felt the psychological and physical pain of this drug and realized that I needed to change this slippery slope that was an unproductive environment.

Back then and still now I don't judge my friends in this community for their choice of this lifestyle. But it was my conscious choice to pave a different path for myself, even if that meant standing out from them and making my own way. I remembered what my mum always used to tell me from the words of the prophet Mohamed: be aware of your companions, friends, and environment, as these will determine your future.

A couple of months later, I broke away from the group and joined a boarding college for the blind in Loughborough with a mixed feeling of anticipation and apprehension. I was excited because it was the perfect environment for me to improve my English and essential employment skills including higher IT knowledge. But I was somewhat nervous because of the flashback memory of what could have been another Al Noor school.

Thanks be to God, none of my concerns of limited freedom materialized. My business administration classes were in a chilled environment with a good balance between extended care and fostering independence. But my next challenge was of feeling excluded because I was Muslim. There were no provisions to allow me to express my faith, including meal choices and being able to observe Ramadan. I also felt obliged to go to nightclubs where alcohol was served.

I learned over time to respect my fellow boarders, to balance my priorities, and communicate my faith to my peers and those working at the college. They fully respected who I was and I began to feel included as a Muslim.

Chapter 8

Itching for Adrenaline

It was at Loughborough, known for its love of sport, that I discovered goalball. I had played in Al Noor but now it became a fascination. Goalball is a paralympic sport that was invented during the Second World War to rehabilitate soldiers who lost their eyesight. It was introduced at the Olympics, in Toronto, in 1976. Played on a gymnasium floor of 18 meters long and 9 meters wide, there are three players in each team with another three sub-players wearing opaque shades. Everyone defends and attacks a 9-meter-wide goal, aided by a tactile floor to help orientate players across the court. We play with a heavy ball with bells in it as we zip this ball across the floor to score points against each other in a match of two halves of 24 minutes.

After a few training sessions, I was invited to take part in my first competitive tournament in Southampton. To my surprise, I was promoted to play in the elite level the next month.

From then on, I realized this sport was going to be a big part of my life.

I started to train hard at the gym and attend all goalball practice sessions. And I took it further when I joined forces with a friend of mine, Ahmed, to establish a registered sports charity known as the London Goalball Club: I was appointed chairman to oversee everything from fundraising, community outreach, and regular training, and national tournaments. Our club emerged from being the weakest team to the most dominant team across the UK, sweeping almost every available trophy. All these achievements achievements, in a short space of time, earned me a call to join the Great Britain squad. During this adventure, I had the pleasure of representing the national team in many international tournaments including the European Championship in Finland, in June 2008.

Then, my involvement with the GB team came to an abrupt end. Since it was announced in 2005, I had a lingering passion to represent the national team at the London 2012 Paralympics. Under my coach, Deena, I had thrived. But when another coach was appointed, we just didn't get on. I was impressed with his eye for detail and learned a great deal from him, but I felt I couldn't tolerate this coach's perceived to be authoritarian—and the subsequent mishandling of resources.

He was publicly rude towards me because I was not afraid to state my opinions. For example, I questioned the absence of any funding for us players. Despite our total dedication to a semi-professional level of training and tournaments for several years, none of us received any monetary compensation. We were expected to put our bodies and mind under great stress for the sake of national pride. Surely no one can sustain living that way without some funding?

I became more resentful of this fact after I got hold of evidence that there was mishandling of the available funding. After raising my concerns formally and informally with no response, I was instead treated with hostility.

By the summer of 2009, it got too much and I rang my coach to resign.

Surprisingly, he urged me to reconsider my decision and join an upcoming tournament in Madrid. In the end, I did play. I wanted to prove that I was a better-than-average player and saved my best-ever performance for that tournament.

I realized then that I am someone who responds well to external pressure. I care about what people think of me and thrive on proving people wrong when I feel they doubt me.

I didn't want to claim that I was a great player. In fact, I was quite an inconsistent one. I learned that

I often fail to show my true potential unless I am challenged enough.

This realization made me understand, I am my biggest enemy in the face of fulfilling my potential, in any area of my life.

But back to goalball. After Madrid, I considered staying with the squad until 2012, but I couldn't morally accept the unfair distribution of resources.

At the age of 26, my ambitions were bigger than goalball, and my body certainly agreed as I couldn't seem to shake off the repetitive injuries of my ankle and wrist.

When my body, mind, and heart gave me collective wisdom, I obliged with a heavy heart. I had to say goodbye to my Paralympian aspirations and I finally withdrew from the national team.

But I still had our local club, and I will always look back at that time with nostalgia and pride. Our club grew quickly in stature and we competed across international club tournaments as well as being selected to upskill the KSA national team through a series of elite sport exchange programs. In just three years, we hit our pinnacle in June 2008, as we hosted our first tournament.

It was amazing to host the tournament, despite our lack of experience and limited resources. And the results were even better! We played with such swagger and cohesiveness that we overpowered every opponent and got to the final.

The highlight was when we played against our arch rival, the West Midlands. We played so well that we had to apply the "Mersey" rule whereby the game had to come to a premature ending because we were ten goals ahead of them. It was the ultimate humiliation, and believe me, we know very well how it hurts as our team had endured the same experience, three years before, at the hands of the very same West Midlands.

Everything was just magnificent on that day from the hosting experience, our unprecedented performance and results, and the passionate speech that I gave in the farewell ceremony for our all-rounder volunteer Michele. It was one of those sunny glorious days.

It is hard to quantify the impact of this sport on my overall development.

From a personal development point of view, it has instilled strong self-discipline in me and propelled my never-give-up spirit, and unleashed my competitive monster. It was a healthy channel to release my stress. I learned to combine physical and mental fortitude to reach optimal performance and this has manifested in helping me feel grounded, gain the ability to recover from defeat and not to rest on my laurels when I am victorious.

It also helped me to be a tenacious-doer; I recall that we managed to undertake, in the Netherlands, a couple of goalball marathons where we played six competitive games in 43 hours with hardly any sleep.

The significant pressure that comes with every detail of the game helps me to thrive under external pressure and deadlines, especially when I feel my back is against the wall.

From a professional point of view, it made me a much more effective team player with a balanced aggression-drive and empathetic approach. I also learned a lot about my moral compass and its importance in guiding the formation of my decisions, no matter what the cost. The club administration responsibility paved the way for my professional future including fostering the skills of business development, PR and communication, budgeting, and event management. I will always be thankful that I found goalball.

Chapter 9

The Pursuit of Belonging and Excellence

A way from goalball and back to the studies. As useful as the vocational course was all round, I wasn't ready to give up academia yet. I once again packed my bags for London, trying to decide the most suitable route to university. I returned to Westminster College to take on an Access course as a foundation to get into university.

But after a couple of months, I unexpectedly withdrew from the course. For strange reasons, I couldn't find my feet in that environment again, something that still baffles me now.

The pressure of the perseverance I had worked so hard to follow suddenly took its toll on me. I now entered uncharted waters of bewilderment and a loss of self-esteem, and remember lying low on the sofa in a flat mental state. I kept telling myself, "You are not good enough to do higher education. You gave up on your dreams at the first hurdle. Most people your age have already graduated from university: what a loser you are!"

I felt like I had hit a dead-end. The streams of my passion started to stagnate and every ambition of mine felt cumbersome.

But as much as my sudden mental fragility was bothering me, I found that there is something comforting in this state of vulnerability. I realized that because of my tough upbringing, I thought and acted in a macho manner for fear of breaking down in the face of adversity. I also realized that I often pursue excellence from extrinsic motives; either to please people or to prove them wrong. It was an eye-opening moment to learn how to fully accept myself for who I am and to operate from intrinsic motivations to be the best version of myself. I learned to detach myself from the expectations of others, and instead, do the best I could for my creator who placed me on this earth with a balanced resource to take one step at a time toward my purpose in this life.

It was a much-needed reflection period where I started to better connect with my own values. I gradually started to take a meta-view of my priorities; focusing on using my strengths without comparing myself to my peers or succumbing to outdated, linear expectations of education and career progression. It meant I had to be patient with my progression and enjoy the experience of studying. It also meant not taking Allah's blessings for granted; everything from my health to appreciating how far I had come, in my 21 years of existence. In practical terms, I learned to widen my mental horizons of what constitutes education and started to volunteer for causes that I was passionate about in the UK, and remotely, in Somalia. I also began to make some tentative plans on adventurous travelling to reignite the missing spark of my zest for life. For my education, this meant embarking on a two-year A-Level course to create a more solid foundation for university. I resisted the temptation to view this move as a step backward, but instead, I viewed it as a necessary crouching to take a higher leap.

In September 2005, I began my A-Level studies at the Royal National College in Hereford. At that time, RNC was the best college for blind people in the UK. The quality of teaching and experience was of a very high standard, attracting both home and international students. I studied my favorite subjects including sociology, psychology, history, and critical thinking. I benefited immensely from the extra support of an, advanced English classes for non-native students. Being in another blind-college for the third time in my life, it was not surprising that my path would inevitably cross with former friends, and I came across again, Edris, from Al Noor, after a gap of seven years. Of course, we spent a lot of time together, remembering our shared childhood memories with a lot of laughter and talk.

Even though the college is situated in a small rural town, I was pleasantly surprised to see integration amongst the students of different cultures. The college reflected that inclusive mindset, although there could have been a better choice of halal meals—we all got fed up with the one frozen dish!

I took full advantage of the activities including horse riding, running, and bowling. By now, the UK really felt like my home and I found myself addicted to the British number-one drug … football. Edris and another friend, Kathryn, introduced me to this highly addictive game that swung me between a cloud of ecstasy before crushing me to the ground in the space of 90 minutes. Kathryn, an avid Everton fan who I knew through goalball, took me to my first live match. When I asked her if David Beckham was playing, she realized that it wasn't just my visual impairment—I knew nothing about the game, saying, "Yahye, this is women's football!" Frankly, it was the first time I knew women competed in the game at international level.

During my second live match, I began to understand more about football culture and it fed my ever-growing football madness. Arsenal was playing at home to Everton in May 2005 at Highbury and demolished Everton 7 – 0. Ever since that day, I have followed almost every Arsenal game on radio or TV and attended dozens of live matches. I bought my own discounted disability membership and began to collect a mountain of merchandise. Even with my limited vision, I find myself highly tuned in to every detail of the match through the commentary services that allows me to "watch" and follow every pass and shot. There is a great level of inclusion provision at Arsenal's stadium, such as discounted tickets for disabled supporters which includes a free pass for a companion as well as the commentary service at the ground for visually-impaired fans.

Oh! Every time I remember the delirious moment when Arsenal scores a goal, with thousands of people shouting in one voice, I get goosebumps!

My obsession with Arsenal had officially begun. I call it an obsession because I found myself highly interested in every detail of my team from the games to the players to the transfers. My mood is dictated by how well or badly they perform. There is a huge culture around football in the UK that is bigger than any religious or political allegiance and I had become part of it.

Arsenal has a special place in my heart, so much so that I wish it had never occupied as I cannot stand such constant and volatile emotions in my life. As football supporters know, we find ourselves emotionally enslaved to the affairs of our beloved teams, spending time and money to keep up with it all—even though those teams are not aware of our existence. It's a welcome distraction from work and study, though, and I believe for many young people the football-drug is a safer addiction than many other types of harmful things that they are exposed to including poverty, violence, and real drugs.

Speaking of my newly shaped culture and identity, in November 2006, I passed the British citizenship test and received my passport. It was a defining moment of true belonging and time to unleash my passion for travelling extensively around the world. Kay at the Royal National College had helped me to prepare for my citizenship test and there is something special to love about her calm and pleasant demeanor; I truly thank and acknowledge her for helping me through the test. As well as the citizenship test, I had also passed my A-Levels with decent grades and was offered a place at a wide range of universities across the UK.

After spending five years in the UK, I felt incredibly happy and proud to legally belong as a citizen. Nevertheless, as a Muslim, I always vehemently condemn the foreign policies of the UK government that breed terrorism and inequality, I have great respect for most of the domestic societal and inclusion policies that makes me a proud British national.

As a Muslim I believe firmly there is no perfect place on earth and the ultimate justice is in the life after. But I cannot hide my disappointment when I see the lack of inclusion and belonging for non-native people in many other countries. To me, the right to belong to where you spend most of your life is the most basic right of being human. I find it unbelievable when someone has no right to belong to the country in which they were born. I am fully aware of the complex societal factors that affect the right of belonging in different countries but on a personal level, I want to express my sincere gratitude for all the education and employment help that I received in the UK and some of the Gulf. I remain hopeful that other countries in the Gulf will take a long-term and sustainable view of the right of belonging. Not only this is the right thing to do, it is essential for developing human potential—arguably the only real resource we have.

Chapter 10

The Educational Keys

The big day that I always dreamt of since I was little had finally arrived. In September 2007, I started my bachelor's degree at Keele University in the Midlands region of England. It may seem somewhat peculiar to overlook other well-known universities in the UK, but Keele university was ranked one of the highest in my chosen discipline of International Relations.

I now embarked on my fourth experience of a boarding education and moved in, yet again, with a new bunch of strangers. But by now, this wasn't what worried me. I was concerned about my English and academic skills. Thank God, I was able to receive a great deal of support to help me with my accommodation and learning, including the support workers who offered accessibility help in class and for reading material. The university had a large number of international and ethnic-minority students, although stoke has a reputation for being a place with radical right-wing nationalist groups. In fact, the university staff held a formal awareness campaigns about this issue for all the non-native white students to ensure we were vigilant outside the premises of the university.

This made me very cautious and I avoided discovering the town that is known as the Potteries. Mostly, I stayed in my room chatting online with friends around the world on MSN or was glued to the football or quiz shows such as The Weakest Link. Every other weekend, I jumped on the train back to London to catch up with my friends. A sarcastic bigot who was a fellow student called them cultural weekends—by now my skin was thick enough that I stood my ground against his prejudice.

But the unthinkable happened. For all of my life, I had dreamed of going to university but I quit after the first year.

It was because of a bizarre situation with the library staff. They repeatedly avoided taking responsibility for making the library accessible to me. When I was firm in asking for reasonable adjustments, they accused me of being rude. For the whole year, I was not provided with a single electronic book that I could access. No effort was made to provide me with alternative accessible reading materials despite my numerous requests and reminders. The library team kept avoiding their responsibility and instead kept referring me to the support workers.

When I was given a verbal warning by the head librarian in their office for being "aggressive", I couldn't accept their lack of responsibility or remorse and I walked away. I would not tolerate the nonsense, no matter at what cost my decision would be.

I felt proud of myself as I walked away from that office. Thinking about it now, I realize I walked away from this state of unacceptable exclusion. Refusing the temptation of falling victim to other people's limitations, I took ownership of the situation and used the gift of choice. For me, it's vital I follow up on my passion irrespective of the cost of my choices. When I find myself excluded or limited, I will spare no fighting spirit to do what I can to change it. But if what I do makes no difference, in a split moment I can follow my intuition to move on.

Life is a constant struggle and it is the wise amongst us who chooses their battles carefully.

That summer, I considered whether I had made the right decision to leave or if I should have challenged the university in court. I realized there was no point dragging myself into a potentially long, legal saga, and instead, I focused my energy on finding somewhere else that would be happy to welcome me and allow me to thrive. Thank God, it was the best single decision that I made in my life that paid huge dividends and helped to shape my future.

After knocking on the door of several universities to join them as a second-year student, I hit the jackpot with the University of Westminster. Even though WU was not known for my subject, it did not matter because of the inclusiveness of the university. Right in the heart of London, at Oxford Circus, the staff at the college were kind and humble and I settled in straight away at this very inclusive institution.

I approached the library hoping for a better luck than at Keele, and was introduced to Claire , the manager of my campus. She and her team were very understanding of my needs and went above and beyond provide reasonable adjustments. They provided me with electronic books and gave me access to a host of journals that I could access independently. They were the ultimate and empathetic professionals who helped me to be in charge of my learning. I wasn't asking for a wish-list, but they provided an honest service and made sure I was fully aware of the services on offer and the support workers who could help me.

I was delighted when I accessed, independently, my first electronic book. I felt free from another layer of disability hindrance and instead was able to focus on learning rather than learning how to learn.

This support had had such a direct result on me that I achieved top top marks at the end of the year. I was awarded a scholarship for my final year and I graduated with a first-class honors degree in International Relations and Applied Translation. It was an incredible milestone that filled my heart with so much joy and pride. At the graduation ceremony, as my name was called, and I walked to the stage to receive my certificate, I was about to burst in to tears. I thought about how hard I had fought to achieve my degree, enduring so much over 20 years in two different countries. I couldn't help but think of my mum who was miles away from me, wishing she could witness the moment, which was the reason that had kept us apart for so long. No family was with me to share that precious day.

Nevertheless, I was grateful to Allah for enabling all the resources and wonderful people who had crossed my path and contributed to my degree success.

If that was the pinnacle of my education excellence, the catalyst of my professional career was soon to follow. I was a member of a list of blind translators and interpreters around the world. Through that email list, I came across a post from a German social enterprise called DSE recruiting for blind trainers in London. It is a unique type of social enterprise that raises inclusion awareness by providing business workshops in complete darkness. It's experiential learning through a role-reversal whereby blind trainers lead workshops for sighted participants from different organizations and corporates. After I was hired, barely two weeks later, I was invited on my first international business trip to Jordan, soon followed by many more trips to different countries across Europe, Africa, and Asia.

I was inspired by this experience to do my master's degree in International HR Management. I realized that I love working with people for a strong cause. Paradoxically, my degree in International Relations also made me understand that the fight for big causes, including poverty reduction and developmental programs, is often intertwined with dirty politics, something I couldn't morally accept.

So I found the HR field with a specialty in the cause of diversity and inclusion an ideal mission for me to pursue. I could be in charge of my moral compass. I applied for a scholarship to do my masters at the University of Westminster while praying for guidance from Allah for this new chapter where everything was happening so rapidly. In a matter of weeks, I had a fully-funded scholarship and a place at the Business School.

I started my MA in September 2010 amidst hectic personal and business travels. As I tried to comprehend my new exciting world, I found myself flat on the sofa again, those strong feelings of self-doubt reappearing. "It took you 20 years to complete your degree, are you really made for MA studies"?

Unlike five years previously, I was not fazed by these emotions. Perhaps it was because I was more mature. Because I am writing this part of the book at the beach, I now stumble across some profound wisdom that I'd like to share. When confronting these types of emotional moments, I have a vivid metaphoric image of an ocean, as if our life resembles an ocean. Like the sea, it is full of mysteries, volatile yet gentle. No matter how long you are on it, one day the ride will be over, so you might as well remember the bigger picture and why you have been chosen to be here in the first place. This temporary nature of the ride inspires us to make the most of it. If we need to survive in it, we need to learn to know when to swim, when to flow, and when to surf above the waves.

I learned that all of us face the emotions of fears, doubts, and sadness. The best way is to surf above or around emotion. This is because emotions are similar to waves, temporary in their nature. We need to understand their important contribution to our lives instead of being fazed by them and allowing them to drain our energy and sink us along the way. To me, swimming is a metaphor for our daily endeavors to make a living: we need to give it our all to make a living but not to the extent we live with exhaustion. Swimming is a skill to be mastered with gentleness rather than sheer willpower. Flowing is the position that resembles the enjoyment of delightful and peaceful moments. Life is just like the ocean, we will fluctuate constantly between these three forms and it's up to us to figure out the intricacies of these fluctuations.

Chapter 11

Countless Blessings

I was blessed beyond words with this generous funding opportunity and it made me more determined to do my best. I kept pondering the fact that were many people from my home of birth who would be prepared to give every bit of their sweat, blood, and tears to be in my position, and yet I could see people around me in the UK were letting opportunities pass them by, and then later, living with regrets. I took so much from this realization.

To my delight, the wonderful Claire (who I'd known previously from Westminster) had been transferred to the Business School in Baker Street, the campus of my MA studies. It was as if she was meant to keep looking after me. As before, she did not spare any effort in providing me with exceptional accessibility support including arranging a dedicated area in the library for me to study with my independent support workers. My appreciation and respect for Claire grew into friendship. I hadn't seen her in the library during the last year of my undergrad and now sadly learned this was because she had been seriously ill. Amazingly, she had completely recovered and after learning how close I had come to losing her, our friendship grew more genuine. I feel so lucky to have met a truly wonderful empathetic and supportive human like her. Without exaggeration, her support for me as a librarian and a friend is a big part of where I am now.

Speaking of friends, let me mention two other wonderful human beings and close friends who I first met when they were independent support workers at the university. Ziad and Ami are two of the reasons I excelled at my undergrad and postgrad. I bonded with them each, in different ways, and, I feel like I have known them forever. Ami was the catalyst for my outstanding academic results as he is the perfect intellectual mate who loves to research and debate. (Since then, he has helped another blind friend of mine achieve his academic dream.) To me, Ami is the perfect mate because I enjoyed being with him both in class and outside: he's an avid reader, a happy-go-lucky dude with a big conscience, and certainly very opinionated. It's no surprise that we really got along. We would spend endless hours at the library, reading and debating away.

Ami was my eyes: he understood me so well that he could write down my words before I spoke them.

Ziad is my great spiritual brother. His is a unique combination of humor, swagger, and deep spirituality, and even though we are quite different in our personalities, we complement each other very well. He was my support worker for a class about Arab identity and the case of Palestine. At the time, he had little understanding of the political landscape and I have always been regular follower of current affairs. On the other hand, I had very little connection with my spirituality while he was Mr Spiritual as a Masters holder of this field. In less than a year, our friendship had grown to powerful inspiration: Ziad joined the largest convoy made of 49 vehicles from the UK to Gaza to relieve the humanitarian suffering in the Gaza Strip in the face of Israeli aggression, in 2009. For me, after spending time with Ziad, I have noticed a big shift in how I react to simple daily things and my new-found ability to tap into a deeper sense of fulfillment with life.

I was further blessed by meeting fellow Somali students, Mohamed Jama and Fatima Haji, who I am both now very close to as well. Mohamed had helped me to reconnect with my Somali community that I had started to unconsciously distance myself from after I first arrived in the UK. Do you remember the group of people who I felt lacked ambition? Yet, I saw in Mohamed a similar passion for education as mine, and a desire to take ownership to build a future of hope.

Fatima had the same qualities. I'll never forget her advice to me some eight years after graduation when our paths crossed again in Dubai when I asked her to help me find a ghost writer to help me with my book. She paused for a second, and told me, "Yahye, nobody in this world can relive your life other than yourself, so go for it and tell your own story in your own words." I literally froze for a little while, and at the same time, felt excited and terrified in equal measure. Every word she said deeply resonated with me: I felt like a timid artist challenged to dare and yet empowered to draw and showcase his own art.

With all this support creating a conducive environment for learning, it should come as no surprise that I passed my MA with flying colours and was presented with an Outstanding Achievement Award. As I received it in the Royal Albert Hall, I felt a strange anti-climax. Despite the moment representing my highest educational attainment, I felt the award deserved to be given to a wonderful fellow student by the name of Tarik. In addition, my focus was on embarking on the next chapter of life because in the same month, I had been invited by the German social enterprise organization, DSE, to join its annual conference in Hong Kong. By then, I had been freelancing for them for about 18 months, and they had invited me to present the findings of my MA dissertation about the impact of their unique business workshop on diversity and Inclusion.

The excitement of those 20 minutes that I spent on stage presenting my findings in Hong Kong, eclipsed my graduation ceremony in London, in all sorts of ways. During the conference, I met a wonderful French lady called Pascale who asked me to share more about my dissertation for her own research. It was a strange meeting, at first, because it highlighted the importance of diversity and inclusion: when she heard I was from Somalia, she immediately asked me about piracy. On one hand, I felt a bit of rage of rage thinking, *Uh-oh, here we go, another stereotyping and negative association of Somalia.* On the other hand, I had a chuckle and realized it was a perfect opportunity to take ownership of an important part of my identity and engage in a meaningful conversation to correct a common misconception.

Over dinner, I told Pascale that yes, my country unfortunately has had an unfair and exaggerated reputation of famine and piracy. The famine is often a result of a seasonal drought whereby the rich livestock and crops become severely impacted and thus people starve. It became a humanitarian crisis during the civil war that since 1990, had destroyed the infrastructure of food supplies and all that ultimately led to a food security crisis. The famine (in the absence of local and international law) then bred piracy. It started as casual attacks until headlines raged after a couple of incidents of foreign ships being held hostage as part of a ransom for money. As the seasonal famine took its toll on people's lives and in the absence of an official government, young people in the coastal areas of Somalia started to act like "navy forces" in response to multinational ships dumping their waste on the coast of Somalia. This careless activity and crime under international law had started to wipe out the abundance of fish in Somalia, thus indirectly exacerbating the famine. While every attack on innocent people should be condemned in the strongest terms, we all need to be mindful of the one-sided media that often portrays a distorted reality of the cause of the unfortunate incidents; ignoring the deeper global inequality between richer countries and those that have been classified as under-developed countries.

Chapter 12
Building Cultural Bridges

Away from controversial political views and moral dilemmas, I believe candid and heart-to-heart conversations, the one that Pascale and I had that night in Hong Kong, is what everyone needs to have more often.

Our views of anything beyond our immediate exposure is often either a stereotype in the absence of knowledge or a distorted understanding of the reality due to biases and news-sensational tendencies from media outlets. Some media companies thrive on sensation and controversy because their success is measured by increasing their viewership ratings, which unfortunately is often achieved through controversy rather than impartiality. While the trend of globalization had increased our interaction with other people, I feel there is a gap in how we all need to solidify our "cultural-competencies" by mutually engaging in meaningful conversations and real experiences to empathize and solve global (and at the same time, local) challenges. My conversation with Pascale was not only a rich cultural-facilitation, but an opportunity to build warm friendships, which resulted in the beginning of my career in Diversity & Inclusion.

There is an untold story between me and travelling. I am not sure if I love travelling because I am making up for the lost 11 years of confinement at Al Noor or if it's something more profound than that, but I am certainly more alive when I am on the go.

To do justice to the 52 countries that I have lived in and visited will require a whole separate book. (Actually, I have a plan to launch a dedicated channel about adventurous and inclusive travelling after the release of this book, so please stay tuned and I'll be grateful for any help and input. In my future engagements with you, you can look forward to so many travelling stories through the eyes of a blind dude.) How I have nearly been shot and arrested in Brazil; stranded in the Arabian desert; my search for my Indian wife in Kerala; who abandoned me in Thailand; experienced an amusing incident with a chicken in Kazakhstan; and hosted 50 strangers, at my house.

One person set me on the course of travelling: Michele. She's the close friend I met through the goalball club as she was the volunteer organizing our training and tournaments. Our first memorable trip was to Majorca in

Spain over the Easter holidays, in April 2006. We were both looking forward to our first holiday with the team yet, in hindsight, there was a clear mismatch between my needs and her expectations. I was a rookie traveller eager for a jam-packed schedule, while she was a veteran traveller who was looking forward to rejuvenating from the demands of a full-time social worker's job.

But Michele understood my enthusiasm and we managed to squeeze in so many activities such as horse-riding and group tours. Everything was almost perfect on that beautiful Spanish island and I loved feeling the white, sandy beach between my toes and tasting the fresh Mediterranean food. My best memory is from a mini musical-show we went to on a boat inside a cave. All in all, it was a lovely holiday where I learned the importance of choosing your travel companion extremely carefully: travelling requires a great degree of synergy that can only be realized through mutual compromise and understanding. This holiday with Michele was the first of more than 10 other international vacations together as well as many other local trips in the UK.

Michele is not only the perfect travel-partner who amplifies my zest for adventures, but she taught me vital traveling skills such as researching, meticulous planning, budgeting and saving. More importantly, she showed me how to respect local culture and not be phased in the face of any unfortunate incidents (we have been robbed and had other travelling disappointments).

I am lucky to have met many wonderful people in my 38 years of existence, but Michele is an exceptionally unique friend who has made me a more rounded human who is able to embrace tolerance and kindness in my interactions with people who are not necessarily familiar to me. She especially helped me with this when I visited her native country, Canada.

From those first holidays with Michele, I have embarked on countless travelling experiences through leisure, business trips, and sports. I learned that there is a huge difference between travelling and tourism. Tourism is often the search for self-gratification and indulgence in as much as possible of self-care. On the other hand, travelling is the quest for personal development where your spirit, mind, and heart, are at the center of the experience rather than your physical needs. In this experience you immerse yourself into the local culture, taking part of different events with people around you. I found myself genuinely appreciating nature and realizing for the first time its importance in sustaining our planet, as well as drawing lessons from how nature deals with adversity while con-tinuously giving in abundance. Adventurous travelling provides me with profound experiential learning to grasp the essence of all human phenomena from physics to politics. I find it the perfect experience to force me to reflect on the perfection of this complex universe: the beauty that we appreciate of the universe, the planet, and life itself must have a creator that made it so beautiful:

it can't be a coincidence. Science is my hobby. I'm not smart enough to be a scientist but I love to watch documentaries: the universe blows my mind. Science is my gateway to the truth, to my faith.

When travelling, you leave behind all your assumptions and the magic of your five senses, your mind and soul take over. You start to observe behaviors, associate phenomena, network with diverse fellow humans and question trends, and experiment without the usual inhibition of routine life. So much has been achieved by people after they have travelled.

Which is my favourite country or city? That's an impossible question! But there are countries that stand out in my memory: Brazil and India are memorable for me for their vast geography from mountains to forests, and also because of the wide range of cultures and customs I enjoyed learning about. Sadly, both countries have something additional in common: I couldn't help noticing the massive gap and disparity between some of the wealthiest people on Earth and the most deprived. This made me understand that every consumption choice each one of us makes each day affects those living in Brazil and India.

Turkey and Egypt captured my imagination with their rich history and incredible cuisines. Just look at how many nations have competed in these lands to make them the home of their civilizations. Malaysia and Canada were another highlight for me: with their diverse populations, both countries provide hope that different people can co-exist in peace. Malaysia is one of the most welcoming countries in the world where citizens of many countries can receive a visa on arrival, and therefore, have a better opportunity to study and work. Canada, with its well-known moderate immigration policies, is leading the way for other wealthy countries to do more about social-cohesiveness.

I'd be a fool if I uphold those two countries as the blueprint of human harmony, nevertheless, I view them as good case studies for when politics revolves around people instead of advancing the agenda of the greediest powerful elites.

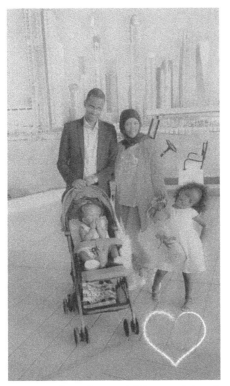

Yahye with his wife and two children celebrating family anniversary in Dubai

Yahye's favourite quote about travelling

Yahye in a panel discussion for early childhood development 2022 summit by the Abu Dhabi government

Yahye receiving his motivational speech award in Muscat Oman

Yahye is running a workshop at Harriet watt university in Dubai

Yahye playing Goalball

Yayhe receiving his top goal scoring medal in Goalball

Yahye riding an elephant in the forest in Thailand

Yahye on a quad bike in Bahrain

Yahye is horse riding in front of the pyramids in Egypt

Yahye standing on a mountain in Bishkek in Kyrgyzstan

Yahye at the cape hope in South Africa

Yahye at Machu Picchu
in Peru

Yahye by a waterfall in Kazakhstan

Yahye is getting ready for scuba diving with his instructor Mike

Yahye is getting ready for Zipline in Kerala, India

Chapter 13

Perseverance with Contentment

My aspirations in the UK were coming to a natural end. As much as I felt at home in England, I had always experienced a value struggle between my ability to practice my faith at ease versus my disability independence (which by the way, are not necessarily mutually exclusive). As a person with a disability, I was unhappy leaving the UK, as I knew wouldn't find in other countries the same level of autonomy. But, at that time in England, there was so much "Islamic-phobia" in the media, creating a direct correlation between Islam and terrorism. In my view, this paradoxically disregarded state terrorism and the intrusive foreign policies of Western countries that fuels the vicious cycle of aggression.

More flippantly, the inconsistent and constantly dark and wet British weather had begun to take its toll on me, and I was ready to chase the sunshine and embark on the next chapter of life adventures.

So, in November 2011, I packed my bags and bought a one-way ticket back to the sunshine of the Gulf. Not only was this a rather bold step, as I had no job offer, but it was a personal challenge to be one of the first blind ex-pats attempting to work in the Gulf region.

I felt strongly about the educational sector, so I made my way to the state of Qatar as there was a lot of talk about bundles of opportunities in this emerging economy. I rented the cheapest hotel room I could find and got in touch with the few people I knew over there. I still remember the shock in people's voices (and I am sure on their faces too) when I approached my target employer, requesting a job. Any real employment opportunities for disabled people in countries such as Qatar are rather scarce: imagine the chances of this audacious blind "alien" getting a job. Despite my slim odds, I kept focused on my task: I would wake up early every morning, jump in a cab, and hop from one organization to the other with my certificates and relentless determination until 4 pm. From 5 pm, I was on my PC applying for as many jobs as possible, online.

I couldn't get a job yet my faith in Allah wasn't affected, in the slightest. As a genuine believer, I know that every bit of blessing that we are aware of (or otherwise) from our health to our wealth, is actually a well calculated supply of "riziq" from the same God who has been supplying the Earth since its inception with all essentials to keep it flourishing. The only way to find out our share of the creator's allocations is to work as hard as possible without losing the internal spirit of contentment with current blessings.

A common trend in my life has been receiving an abundance of blessings from the least expected source—a lesson written in the Quran. As I reconnected with Pascale over email, I mentioned that I was looking for a job. She arranged an interview with the largest media outlet in the MENA region, MBC Media-Group, headquartered in Dubai. As part of the company's expansion, they were looking for people to fill several HR roles. I conducted my interview over the phone but didn't think I'd done very well as most of the interview questions were centered around my ability to turn up independently to the office as a blind person.

To my surprise, a couple of weeks later, I received a job offer of a three-month contract as HR Coordinator.

I snatched this opportunity with both hands and teeth! I viewed the short-term contract as an opportunity to prove myself in this company or use it as a spring-board to propel my career. I was not oblivious to the understandable hesitation of this company to employ me as they had never previously hired a blind person. It was a mutual responsibility: it was my share of responsibility to accept this limited contract in order to showcase my potential and ultimately encourage more hiring of people with disabilities. The three-month contract meant I felt there was no pressure and if it didn't work out, I was free to leave. *Just go for it*, I thought! I always had the idea I wanted to work in the education sector in A teaching, research or lecturing capacity. But suddenly I was working for a media company—using the skills I had learned but didn't expect to use. Was someone like me cut out for a media company? I constantly tried to prove myself: there was minimal adjustment so I took my own personal laptop to work and used that for the first couple of weeks before the accessible software was uploaded. I needed to prove I could do the job despite my disability. My boss had to take me seriously before even considering whether I could do the job and everyone had much curiosity about the basics: How was I going to turn up to work? How will I find my seat when I got to the office? How will I send an email? But I was independent. I had to work twice as hard for every step to prove myself.

I started my job in January 2012, determined to make the most out of the opportunity while enjoying cosmopolitan Dubai and the abundance of sunshine that I had dearly missed. MBC certainly looked after me and made my transition pretty straightforward: they offered me a fully-furnished apartment in a beautiful green neighborhood community and a decent salary for a young graduate. What also made the transition into ex-pat life in Dubai easier was meeting one of my now best friends,

Mahmoud, within a few days of my arrival. To me, he is "the brother from another mother" with big heart and zest for life. I met him at the Metro train when he approached me, offering to help a lost blind dude who was visibly standing out in the crowd with his white cane. We were heading in the same direction, literally and metaphorically: I was practicing the route of getting to work before my first day. That first journey together allowed us to get to know each other well. The next day, he helped me move from the hotel to my new apartment and from there it felt that we been known to each other forever.

About the same time, the wonderful Pascale invited me for a Boxing Day dinner, at her house with her husband, Sam, and two children. Before going around, I popped into the local mall to fetch a couple of items: in our Somali and Arabic culture, it is part of the gathering courtesies never to turn up to your host empty-handed. As usual, I was running late, so Sam had come directly to the mall to pick me up. I was rather embarrassed as I needed to go back to the apartment to change my clothes. He gladly offered me a ride home and helped me with a couple of chores while I was getting ready. Finally, I was ready and during the car journey to his house, we began to chat properly. I asked him what he did at MBC: he replied that he was the CEO. I froze in astonishment and admiration: he had been so humble and yet, was a great leader. It was a lovely dinner with him and Pascale, and one of several together that we enjoyed.

The weeks in Dubai began to fly by, and my circle of friends continually grew. I discovered hiking and camping at weekends. And at work, I had impressed my employer so that my contract was converted to a permanent employee. It felt like my journey of perseverance was complete. After all those years, my education had led to a tangible outcome. I believe I was the first blind ex-pat in Dubai, maybe in the whole of the Emirates, to work. I saw a lot of ex-pats in Dubai but none with a disability. Some Arabs with a disability are employed but usually just to fulfill a national quota or as part of Corporate Social Responsibility.

I felt as if I had made it on my own merit and it really made me proud. I had to pinch myself sometimes to see if it was all real: everything was happening so fast I couldn't comprehend it but by the summer of 2012, I felt quite settled in my job, and I received a very strong calling to reconnect with my family back in Somalia. By then, I hadn't seen my parents and siblings for 22 years. It was an extraordinarily long time. I rang my mum and told her how much I missed her and how I couldn't bear the separation any longer. Out of care for my safety, she told me she wasn't sure I should visit Somalia because of safety reasons. I knew she was just happy to know that I was doing well and that she didn't want me to be exposed to any danger that I was not familiar with. But I insisted on visiting her, as finally, I had the financial means and the time to do so.

With the support of my friend Mahmoud, I booked my ticket to Mogadishu for the last couple of days of Ramadan and Eid al-Fitr.

Chapter 14

Where Am I?

I am going down the stairs of the airplane at Mogadishu, feeling a gentle breeze, pleasant drops of rain, and quite mild weather. I was really shocked and for a second, I thought I had landed in the wrong country. It was mid-August and so I expected Somalia to be very hot similar to Dubai. Of course, this was ill-informed thoughts that derived from the media; that the whole of Africa is hot. But perhaps more importantly, this moment confirmed how much I have been disconnected from my roots. As I approached the bottom of the stairs of the airplane, I suddenly felt a strong shove on my arm. In a moment of naivety, I was scared and my thoughts jumbled: *Was I getting kidnapped? Or experiencing some of the violence that I'd heard about in Somalia?*

It was my second oldest brother, so excited to welcome me back with a big hug!

The airport was a small building, and fortunately, I had one of my best friends from Al Noor with me, Ibrahim, to help translate what the immigration officials were asking. I could feel the atmosphere was tense and there were heavy security controls.

It's sadly true that I had forgotten almost every word of Somalian, my original mother language. The magnitude of realizing that I couldn't communicate in my native country was bigger than anything else I had experienced as an adult. I felt such shame and guilt.

As we left the airport, even with my limited vision, I noticed the destruction of the war apparent everywhere. Our hire car forced its way through roads that were almost totally destroyed. My mind raced through terrifying thoughts, *Would be ambushed? What about land mines?* Thank God, all these fears remained hypothetical and we reached our home safely.

I got out of the car and hazily saw my mum standing in front of our modest house. I felt numb. It was a miracle that we were finally together after 22 years.

I stood in front of her like a statue, in total shock and disbelief to be reunited. She was in a fragile physical condition, and yet, still so full of energy. My only regret now is not going down on my hands and knees and kissing my mother's feet out of admiration.

It felt as if I'd travelled back in time to the same house from all those years ago—except it was a house that had degraded in 22 years, with a third of it destroyed after a rocket hit it during the peak of the war.

Ibrahim realized how deeply I was affected by this moment and so made me laugh to break the tension. He welcomed us all with great enthusiasm and my mum had then prepared for me a feast of Eftar to break our fast upon sunset. Remembering the simple ways of life in Somalia brought me down to earth; a bucket of water for bathing and no electricity were a contrast from my swanky lifestyle in Dubai and London. But to put it simply, nature is at its best with simplicity. I realized that the more I had, the more stress I had. Like all of us, I selfishly do whatever it takes to accumulate more material belongings to feel happy. And, yet, many of us develop isolation, depression, and other mental health issues because of our attachment to material things and the insecurity of losing what we have accumulated. Human psychology means that the grass is always greener on the other side of the fence. But the happiest amongst us are those who live with contentment and are fulfilled by a purpose that is bigger than ourselves.

My friends and family spared no effort in offering me the best they could, from the choicest food to the best sleeping spot, to avoid mosquitoes. Even with my mum's physical fragility coupled with her high blood pressure, she would constantly take care of me, a grown adult, day and night. Just as when I was a child, I noticed she always put my desire above her own needs.

It wasn't just me. She woke up in the middle of the nights to attend to her crying grandkids then, soon after, would wake up at dawn to cook breakfast of liver with bread and milk the camel. Life for her was to constantly carry out family and community tasks in-between cooking lunch of camel meat and rice and then dinner—a Somali traditional supper of either suqar (small pieces of meat) with mofo (a type of bread), or ambula—a type of bean with sugar and thick oil.

There is nothing in this life that can replace the compassion of a mother, either in the world of humans or animals. That is, other than the one who placed this compassion in their hearts in the first place to keep the pulse of our life ticking—our God.

Ibrahim stayed at our house to translate for me. I was doing my best to avoid admitting the sad reality that I was talking to my own mother through an interpreter. It was bizarre beyond imagination. I felt as though I was a representative of a UN mission rather than a loving son at home with his mother.

My mother and I were both grateful to His Mighty for our reunion after such a long separation. Mum had not only endured the pain of the separation from me and my older sister (who was in the States), but she had survived the devastation of the brutal war. Almost as bad, she had also denied for 22 years gross and vulgar accusations from local women. I learned they had spread rumors that my mother had sold me to rich Arab people, as they simply didn't believe the truth that I had won a scholarship to Al Noor. The women said it was the reason why our family had enough money throughout the years I had been gone.

My mother wasn't interested in proving a point to anyone but it was important to her that she and our family regained credibility in our community. So, she invited to our house the women who had spread the rumors so they could see me alive and free from any foreign ownership. My mother wanted every member of our family to live with a clean reputation and to leave an impactful legacy after death.

I will always remember fondly those precious hours I spent in my mum's company listening to so many stories that I had missed over the years. One of them was rather embarrassing but it explains my feisty character. She told me that when I was barely five-years-old, I went with her to her butcher's stall at the local market. As she was entertaining some lengthy conversation with her customers, I got bored and decided to find my own entertainment. There were no children in the near vicinity to play with, so I decided to roll over in the sand. One of the women talking to my mum sneered at me, calling me dirty and full of sand. Apparently, I dusted myself off, puffed out my chest, and replied, "Ooohhh! Look who is calling me dirty? You forgot that your hair was so dirty yesterday, I saw women helping you pick the lice out of it!"

Although I felt embarrassed at being so rude to an adult, my mum said she had been secretly proud of my character. She told me that she knew then I would be the sort of person who would survive anywhere because I could stand up for myself. It got me thinking about other situations throughout my life when I had acted in a similar way, including some of the stories I've told you in this book. It made me realize that I have a raw tendency to denounce any form of bullying or injustice of any sort. A consistent theme in my life is that I am someone who wears his heart on his sleeve. I always say what is in my heart, or at least, it will show on my face. I find it hard to tolerate any nonsense that harms another person, especially when it comes from someone in a position of status.

I have walked away from so many places and abandoned friendships when I saw an injustice or exclusion—even if it resulted in relinquishing a big opportunity or a financial loss. I find myself driven by morals, ethics, and values of inclusion, fairness, and empathy: I'll do whatever it takes to defend these principles. My feisty response as a five-year-old kid represented a kind of pure and unfiltered version of confronting unfairness. As I got older with age and experience, I became more calculated about what is worth fighting for, ignoring, or simply walking away from.

Chapter 15

A Day Dream

My mum's stories made me cry, her words filling my heart with feelings and my mind with realizations. The reality of what war had been like for her was shocking: in order to survive, her tribe had appointed its own security force and two of my brothers were defending our village. People had taken the law into their own hands with casualties on all sides. Mum said she was able to bear the civil war until in 2006, when she had no choice but to finally flee her house. She lived in the middle of heavy artillery fights between Somalia and the forces of Ethiopia, the neighbouring country, and the local Islamic Court government at that time. This led to mass destruction of Somalia: a third of our house had been destroyed, but, thanks be to God, no casualties in my own family. I was devastated to realize what she and my family had gone through. It disgusted me that those innocent people in Somalia and other places around the world are forced to pay the price of war.

Mum told me that she coped by trusting God. She learnt how to survive with so much insecurity by living her life moment by moment. Every time someone from the family went away, she would kiss their head, saying, "I leave you in the hands of Allah." She could never be certain they would return alive. She told me that second to Allah's blessing, she had survived because of me, because of the money I had sent from my wages in the UK. To hear these words from my mum overwhelmed me. It made me realize God's wisdom in our long separation. It made me understand there is always a reason for events that happen to us—it is not just random chance. Sometimes, we might immediately realize the reasons for incidents, or it might take us a few months or years, or even generations through historical evidence, to find out.

I believe it is not important to seek an explanation for what we go through, but rather to achieve a balance between non-passive acceptance and genuine contentment for whatever is beyond our understanding and control. We must work towards the best intention and effort to make a positive impact on our lives.

The morning of Eid-Alfiter, we all woke up for dawn prayer, put on new clothes, as is tradition, and made our way to the mosque. My mum had invited many relatives to join us, as well as all of our neighbours those women who spread rumours about her. It was a double celebration for her—celebrating Eid and her reunion with me.

People came to the mosque in large numbers to see this 'Yahye' who had returned after all these years. I could see the joy and pride I had brought to my family for what God had helped me to accomplish abroad. Yet, I was miserable because I couldn't talk to anyone in Somalian. One of my brothers teased me, calling me "ajnabi"—the foreigner.

You might question why I haven't mentioned my beloved father. We'd been in regular communication all the time while I was abroad and I loved him dearly. But there was unfortunate friction between him and the rest of my family. He and my mum had separated and my father now had formed another family.

When I had first heard about the separation, it made me rather sad. I felt trapped between both of my parents. But I came to understand the view from each side and was able to maintain a good relationship with both of them. Because I had been away for many years I wasn't interested in digging for problems that were beyond my capability to solve, but during my one-week visit to Somalia, I feel as if I went some way to reconciling my parents. My dad and some of my siblings spoke to each other after a long time of no communication. My dad agreed to come and visit us at home, and that, in itself, went a long way in the mediation. I was so thrilled to meet him again. We talked and he offered me much advice and wisdom, including about my future financial investment and, as I was now thinking about the next stage in my life, getting married.

I had been in Somalia less than a week and couldn't speak Somalian yet I had already connected with my roots. I found myself arguing with my siblings about their reliance on my mum. She had worked so hard for so many years and had earned the right to put her feet up. But my younger sister was the only one who was helping with a responsibilities of the house. My oldest sister has a visual impairment like me. She was resilient and content with her life but it was sad to see her lack of independent life skills. My oldest brother is visually-impaired, as well, but was living separately with his own family. Three of us were living abroad: my second oldest sister was in the USA; and my second youngest sister, had been in Sweden for several years by then.

All the siblings had learned to live the life of their choice and make the most of it, regardless of their location or resources in life. My mum's biggest concern wasn't about her deteriorating health but instead doing whatever she could to secure a happy future for her children, locally, and around the world.

Apart from the first morning of Eid, I only left the house once in six days when Ibrahim took me to visit the local visually-impaired school where he was working. The school was sponsored by a powerful telecommunication company as part of their CSR initiatives; I thought that was quite impressive for a country that learned to function for so many years without a government.

As we finished our visit, we went into the city with one of my brothers—despite the strict warning from my mum not to do so because it was unsafe. As we took pictures of the local government building, we nearly got shot for breaching the security rules. But when the security guards discovered who our mother was, fortunately for us, her good standing meant we were let off with a warning. We made our way to Lido Beach in Mogadishu, well-known in Somalia for its historical and cultural significance. The place was full of local kids, men, and women, as well as many returning Somali diaspora. We again took another huge risk by hanging around that area and eating in one of the local restaurants. The place had been blown up many times by radical groups.

As we made our way back home we drove just next to the convoy of the newly-formed government; thank God we passed unscathed as the area is often extremely dangerous. The Al-Shabaab group vehemently opposed any government that was assembled under the approval of the international community and frequently attack it. When I got home, the tension continued because my uncle had been to visit: Mum had told him not to return while I was there. I didn't understand why and my mum wouldn't tell me. I learned, years later, from my youngest sister, when I visited her in Sweden, that my uncle was a senior figure in the Somali government who was openly opposing Al-Shabaab. My mum didn't want any danger at home while I was visiting as my uncle often publicly announced the justice verdict of members of Al-Shabaab who killed many innocent people. Unfortunately, and as is the case with anyone who works for the government, he was assassinated by Al-Shabaab, a couple of years later.

Those six days at home had felt to me like six years because of the wealth of wisdom and insights I had gained, the people I had met, and the connections I had made. When it was time to go home, it was awful to have to say goodbye to my mother again—not knowing if and when we would see each other again. She had devoted her life to me and my siblings and I could never thank her enough. A few years after we said goodbye, I was able to show her my love in a small way.

I had tried to convince her many times to allow me the honour of funding her trip to perform the Haj pilgrimage. She would always politely refuse as she felt she couldn't leave her mother at home, who was very ill. When her mother sadly passed away, I made the offer again and after several more times of begging her, she said yes. My oldest brother accompanied her in 2013. I never felt as proud of anything in life as much as I felt, in that moment. The Haj-pilgrimage is the ultimate honor of any Muslim and the pinnacle of the religious point for which we all strive. I felt it was the least I could do, to modestly thank my mum for everything she has done for me. It represents the most precious and proudest moment of my life, so far.

But as I left my family home for the airport to return to Dubai with my friend Ibrahim, my brother, and my sister, I had no choice but to bid my mother farewell. As the plane took off and climbed higher in the sky away from Africa towards the Middle East, I tried to comprehend the magnitude of the visit. I felt as if I was high above the clouds to meta-view my life, celebrate the past, feel grateful for the moment and embrace the future with all its mysteries.

What I had experienced during those six days in Somalia was profound for me on every level of emotion, intellect and spiritual connection. I felt as if I had read endless, books and lived every moment of deep life lessons. The only way to describe the experience was that it was out of this world and the most important week of my life so far. My connection with God had grown stronger as I felt, for the first time, I was being driven by a bigger purpose in this life.

Chapter 16

When There is a Will, There is a Way

I returned to Dubai and resumed my life there. I was constantly socializing, losing sleep, and putting on the pounds until I realized I needed something to refocus my life again. Out of nowhere, the answer came. Mike was an Italian friend of mine and he sent me a message on Facebook: "Yahye, I have an amazing offer for you that you cannot refuse!" It turned out that this engineering graduate, who worked as a professional chef, was training to be a scuba diving instructor with the Jumeirah Group. The dive center was launching the first diving program for people with disabilities and Mike wanted me to join in.

I was baffled at first: I had genuinely never heard of scuba diving before. Africans tend to stay on the land rather than the sea! I couldn't swim. But frankly, this is what made the adventure even more appealing to me. I love to push my boundaries and Mike knew how crazy I am for new adventures—the stranger, the better!

The first day, I turned up at the center and Mike introduced me to the wonderful Elena: she was the other instructor and in charge of looking after me. I was nervous, confused, and rather fascinated as she explained about all the equipment and gear I would be using—especially the weird long swimming flippers. But Elena was sweet and gentle, reassuring me that everything would be fine: she was the total opposite of Mike who kept pressing every button of mine that responds to challenges. Between them, and with God's help, something magic happened. During my third session, I suddenly felt relaxed as I lay in the swimming pool, surrounded by water that I couldn't see. During that session too, I felt comfortable putting on the gear myself. When I asked when we would be practicing in the ocean, Elena and Mike told me to slow down! The thing I loved about the program was the creative way it made scuba diving possible for people with disabilities. The biggest hurdle for a blind person under the water is how to communicate with their buddy. There is a significant risk of taking someone with a disability out scuba diving but it was not an issue with Mike and Elena. They introduced me to sets of tactile communications and arm gestures so I could communicate under the water about ascending, descending, equalising, swimming, and stopping.

I found myself falling in love with scuba diving. It started to fill the void that goalball had left. The amazing program had attracted the attention of newspapers and TV stations and I conducted many interviews about my adventure, and the unique inclusive initiative. My own media employer was one of the first to interview me on Sabah Al Khair ya Arab, one of their most followed morning shows.

As the weeks passed, I passed the theoretical exam with relative ease but I almost failed the practical one. If it wasn't for Mike, who was my examiner, bullying me along I doubt that I would have passed. It was an exciting, fun initiative and I realized I was living my motto in life: when there is a will, there is a way. I learned it from my mother and have always used it throughout my life. I am an outsider in many ways because of my diversity: I have faced and will continue to face endless challenges against many odds. Believing and living with my motto is hard work but I would never have it any other way.

Teaching non-disabled persons scuba diving is a hard job, so imagine adding to that someone who is blind and does not know how to swim. But all of us had a strong will to succeed and we found a way. The diving-center benefited from well-earned publicity, Mike built his new career, I learned a new set of skills, and the local media beefed up their content with a new dimension.

Imagine if every organization and their colleagues applied such a collaborative and inclusive mindset in order to propel their inclusion agenda. It requires creativity and ignoring the fear of failure that so often curtails imagination and potential. Thank you, Mike and Elena, for proving that when there is a will, there is a way.

Chapter 17

The Dichotomy of Authenticity and Diversity

The trip back home to Africa had been such a joyous time that I decided to meet the only member of my family I hadn't seen as an adult: my second youngest sister, in Sweden. The last time we saw each other had been 23 years previously. As I stood in the middle of the train station in Stockholm, I suddenly felt a tight hug. It was my sister: she had always been affectionate. Imagine if it had been a random tipsy female enjoying the Swedish mid-summer festival, showing a lonely blind dude some love! Joking aside, it didn't take long for her and me to resume our bantering and messing around in her flat. Within a few hours, we were laughing and arguing with each other, as though we had never been apart.

The rest of my family aren't as physically affection-ate but I have no doubt of their love. It made me realize that people express their feelings in different ways—especially older people and in more traditional cultures, it is important not to confuse lack of physical touch as harshness or lack of emotion.

Speaking of love, it had come to the point when I became interested in finding a special person to spend the rest of my life with. My close friends knew that I had been involved in a few relationships with no intention of marriage. My life was a train running 100 miles per hour, moving from one country to the other, and so were my relationships. But not only was that behaviour not in accordance with my faith, but it was also at odds with my character of commitment.

In our culture, marriage is viewed in quite pragmatic terms, as the best investment every person should strive to make. This is not to dismiss the importance of love and romance, but it's more about the bigger picture of the marriage. This is also supported by the teachings of our Islamic religion that every "capable" person should seek marriage. The criteria of capability include health, finances, and a willingness to settle down. There is no harm if couples get to know each other prior to the marriage as long as their relationship is not secretive and does not break the modesty of verbal or physical contact of any sort. Our marriage structure also means that two different families will bond, so it is vital to find a compatible partner with the same values in life. While there is no harm in pursuing someone for their physical appearance, brains, or financial stability, the most important criterion should be inclusive of religious and good character.

I believe that love and romance will develop out of a compatible marriage rather than being a prerequisite to it. Many relationships and marriages quickly break down if a couple naively expects the romance that bonded them in the first place to remain throughout the relationship. A relationship is just like anything else: rather fluid, and thus it goes through different forms and stages of development. Each stage has its own unique moments that are relevant to that particular time. In my view, the reason that marriage is the most suitable way to engage in a relationship is that it fosters love and commitment of equal measure. Marriage creates understanding and acceptance as it develops throughout the years.

In terms of the method of choosing a partner, Islam does not dictate one particular way. It could be an individual's pursuit or the introduction by a family member or friend. Arranged marriage is a cultural tradition rather than religious practice. And, as much as the family and the community's input of a particular couples' choices should be welcome, the ultimate decision must be in the hands of the couple themselves.

I like the middle-ground that Islam takes on marriage as well as many other things. In some other religions, marriage becomes a life sentence whereby it's forbidden to divorce no matter the ramifications of a given toxic and harmful relationship. Other practices go to the other extreme side of the spectrum, whereby relationships resembles a revolving door with no intention to commit. According to Islam, if a marriage breaks down, the first level of solution should be between the partners and only where necessary will the family and community's intervention be required to reconcile between those partners as the second level of mediation. If the situation between the couples is becoming untenable, then the option of divorce will be exercised, as the absolute last result. Even after the divorce, both divorcees must attend to their financial and social responsibilities, as well as custody of any children.

The essence of the above, and in fact the essence of this entire book, can be captured in two words, intention and intuition. Everything in life is possible if we take care of the purity of our intention. Once we hold the space of our intention, we will receive powerful intuition to guide us in the path of life.

At school and university, we are taught plans and strategies to shape the perfect life; they are important, but I believe they are far from being enough without a solid foundation. Planning and strategizing are tools that often are out of our influence, and more importantly, cannot reflect the fluidity of the "being" that characterizes our humanity. In other words, we need to master the most powerful tool in life, that of intention, to then receive the light of intuition so we can ultimately "see" the way for planning and strategizing. Pure intention is the gift of life that every human is born with irrespective of background and status. It is the bedrock and software of every move and action in life.

My mother taught me that intention is what we are fully in charge of. The outcome of anything, is in the hands of the creator, irrespective of the perfection of our plans.

After my family reunion in Somalia, I felt a grounded and beautiful reconnection with my roots, and this connection had, in turn, allowed me to finally embrace my identity and faith. As a young kid who grew up away from his family and culture, I found myself more often than not behaving in any necessary but disingenuous way to fit in with different environments and people. Worse than that, I found myself in a total identity crisis because of my diverse background. I would often unconsciously disguise my Somalian heritage and my faith, so I could appeal to the approval of others. My identity crisis had become a cultural homelessness.

One morning in Dubai, I was sipping on a cup of coffee, gazing with my limited sight at a palm tree through my balcony. I pondered on the gentle fluctuation of this tree's branches in the face of the wind while remaining firmly rooted on the ground. I saw it as a metaphor for my life: I was living in an inauthentic way. The purest version of myself was screaming with the loudest voice possible, asking me, "What's the point of this pretentious life? Has God chosen you to have an opportunity on this earth to be an actor?"

The thought shook me and I woke up to the reality that most of the pretentious behavior I was displaying was to fit in with others. The strongest connections and most meaningful relationships I had in my life were possible because I stood tall with all the different facets of myself. There was no point in my rich diversity if I was going to hide it whilst making entertaining chit-chat at dinner tables. My soul was starved of authenticity.

Deep down, finding a partner excited and intimidated me in equal measure. But a clear pattern for my life has been a tendency to follow my intuition and then act rapidly on something that has been on my mind. So it was in Sweden, that online, I met the great love of my life, my wife, Deeqa. I was staying at my sister's flat and when I checked my Facebook one day, I had a message from a random girl. Actually, she wasn't that random at all—I had asked my friend, Mahmoud, a few months before, to put me in touch with any decent female friend he knew. I had begun to think about settling down and wanted to meet a nice girl. We exchanged a few messages and planned to see each other.

Deeqa lived in Abu Dhabi, so when I went home, we met. It was 6 July 2013, at the bus station. I was pretty nervous as we shouldn't have been meeting alone, really.

But, I will never forget the first time I heard Deeqa's voice; she said, "Hi, it's me." Her voice was soft. It was lovely, and instantly, I found it sexy. It was tantalizing in my head to imagine her. I could tell she was shy: I wasn't interested in how she looked, more about how she felt. I hoped she wasn't too skinny or too fat. We all have our biases! It was in that moment that the difference between sighted people and blind people and non-visual preferences come into place: I wasn't bothered about how she looked as long as she had a non-rough voice.

As we drove away in her car, it felt so romantic. I cannot drive and to find a female friend who wants to drive me on a date with her, was a wonderful feeling. If it had been simply a friend offering me a lift, I would've felt my independence compromised and suggested I took public transport instead. But I knew Deeqa was special. Even now, when she makes me a cup of tea and brings it into me while I'm working, it's the most romantic thing ever. If someone offers me one in the office, it doesn't feel the same.

As Deeqa and I talked during that first meeting, we both knew we were serious about our intentions. I had found my faith, I knew what I was clear about and knew how I should act. For Muslims, it is God first, family second, and work third. With that in mind, when you love somebody, I knew I would love them for the sake of God. That is what would make me a better Muslim and a gentleman. I wanted to do what was right and the question was to find somebody who fitted that ideal. But it had to be someone I had chosen. I didn't want a product from a shelf. I wanted to marry a compatible human being: we both wanted to make sure marriage was our choice.

We had to be interested in each other without any external influences.

Chapter 18

Forming the Nest

In the search for my true self, I understood that I needed to purify my intention to pave the way for a happy future. From this pure intention, I landed the intuition that Deeqa is God's choice to be my love, my wife, and the mother of my children.

Thank God, she was also pure and clear in her intention to get married.

It took six months of talking about the practicalities of getting married before we broke the news officially to her family. Since my immediate family is scattered all over the world, I informed my far-flung relatives that I needed their support to formally approach Deeqa's family. In our culture, once a couple would like to marry, the proposal follows a formal approach between the two families.

So, 14 members of my relatives agreed to join me and form an official marriage proposal delegation to Deeqa's family. Unfortunately, Deeqa's family resisted me. Partly because of my disability, and partly because I come from a different tribe.

Unfortunately, both reasons are common issues in our society even though are in contradiction with our religion that has clear anti-discrimination policies.

My background was being thoroughly checked, and Mahmoud was my principle reference as my unofficial matchmaker: we all live and die by our reputations. Our assembled mini convoy of 14 delegates arrived at Deeqa's family's house to present the formal marriage-proposal and to request her hand. The delegates were received with generous hospitality and the oldest members of both sides lead the negotiations. For me, it was a rather annoying experience. Not only because of the excessive formalities, but I was also literally lost in translation due to my poor Somali language. I kept biting my nails, especially as the discussion became more heated in relation to what appeared to be certain expectations.

My delegates made their case as strongly as they could and Deeqa's family promised to talk to us within a week, after more checks on my character.

Deeqa and I were very clear about our mutual commitment, so we were in no doubt of our choice of each other but we still needed the blessing of our families. During the week, while I was waiting for an answer, I heard so many rumours about me in the community. The funniest one was that I was a rich blind guy in his 60s with Mahmoud as my official account manager. One of the saddest was people questioning my ability to look after a family: "He couldn't even see the cup of tea that was placed right in front of him on the table. How he is going to take care of your daughter and their kids?"

As much as I was disheartened by such ignorance, I knew this was just another example of ignorance that derives from a lack of interaction with persons that have a disability. Assumption and judgement were influencing these people rather than a healthy curiosity and appropriate questions. Luckily, my history of independence and achievements were the best answer to their doubts. I didn't say anything but let my life speak for itself.

Emotional reactions can fuel perceived doubts, and I learned that when someone patronizes me, they are in essence only patronizing themselves. The perceived limitation that some people place in their minds about my abilities is nothing more than a reflection of their limited capacity to understand. And their limitation does not determine my potential.

My focus was never about gaining Deeqa's family's approval for the sake of it, but instead, I was seeking to form a beautiful family with their daughter who loves me for who I am. As Muslims, we look to seek the approval of God above and beyond his creatures. From this place of authenticity, I took much comfort and was able to better deal with this situation.

I hadn't informed my parents as I knew that they would trust my judgement in choosing Deeqa. But when I realized how strong the disapproval of Deeqa's family was, I called my mum. Tough times require tough people and she had always been there for me. A few phone calls later, we received the approval of Deeqa's family. We were both so relieved and happy as we didn't want to form our marriage at the cost of falling out with her family.

With the green light, the wedding preparations began. Normally, the cultural tradition involves many financial agreements of all sorts between the bride and her family including a set of jewellery and cash gifts to be distributed among the attending family members during the ceremony. As a part of Somalian cultural tradition, this cash is known as "Suriad" and it has to be wrapped in a piece of cloth that is usually worn on the head. All these are cultural norms and must not be confused with religious prerequisites.

The religious requirements are limited to a "Maher"—a reasonable financial allowance that the man pays to the woman. Culturally, this Maher has an advance amount and deferred amount (in the unfortunate case of divorce). In fact, the Maher itself is optional while at the same time being an entitlement: the bride can exercise the right to let go of it or demand it as a prerequisite of the marriage. Islam recommends that the less the Maher, the more blessing the marriage will be. This recommendation is to prevent the marriage from becoming a lucrative business deal and ensuring the whole thing is not built on debt. During the ceremony, couples must give clear verbal consent in the presence of Maathoon, a religious figure, as well as in front of the bride's custodian and two witnesses.

A few days after an Islamic marriage ceremony is an official court ceremony. This is to further guarantee the right of the bride as the marriage will be registered and recognized by the local and international civil law with an official marriage certificate. Interestingly, our court registration is subject to presenting a marriage medical certificate. This medical result is to scientifically predict the level of genetic compatibility between a couple. Based on scientific compatibility, the test predicts the likelihood of a clash of genes that might result in a disability of the couple's children.

I like this procedure, not only because of the power of making an informed decision but because my visual disability and two of my siblings' are as a result of incompatible genes. While this topic is complex and I would never swap my own blessed life despite my blindness, I feel that, in general, it is always better to be informed. This is crucial to be able to live in peace with the choices that we made in life, rather than to live with regret and anxiety by dismissing available options.

In either case, divine contentment is required to guide our state of being and doing. While it is a lot easier to think this way rather than to feel it, I believe that we can realize this fulfilling state of being when we are connected with God. Regardless of how hard we tend to subconsciously let control go, the divine knows better than humans can ever know. The state of deep contentment and letting go is the Arabic linguistic meaning of the word Islam.

Ironically, the beauty of our limited knowledge as humans, is what propels us toward continuous learning and discoveries. So, this confirms that the beauty of being human, manifests itself through the state of imperfection while perfection is the divine right of God alone.

Chapter 19
Colorful Memories

After intense preparations, our wedding day arrived, coming only four weeks after our ceremony. Deeqa and I didn't want to drag things out and risk letting unexpected issues get in the way. Religiously, we could have moved in together right after the ceremony but culturally, the bride should leave her parent's house, and move to her husband's home after the wedding party.

I always wanted to enjoy a spectacular wedding even though it would mean a great cost. While Deeqa equally wanted a special wedding, she was considerate about the financial implication. I appreciated her thoughtfulness. Luckily, my father's advice to be financially smart, meant that I could finance the day without breaking the bank.

Our wish for a spectacular wedding could not have been realized better without the incredible support of my wonderful matchmaker, Mahmoud. He worked as a full-time wedding planner for a month on top of his regular job. He recruited twelve of our friends to form a dancing band to perform at the wedding and turned my flat into a dancing studio for their practices. He hired a limousine to travel from Dubai to the wedding venue in Abu-Dhabi. It was an amazing atmosphere of exuberant celebration. Our friends surprised us with another gift, which was a limousine pick-up and drop between the hotel and venue. Mahmoud also gave me wedding clothes—a full suit and another full set of luxurious Arabic dress including a bishet (a formal and elegant cover from the shoulder to the ankle).

From the moment Deeqa and I stepped out of the limousine into the reception, it was spectacular. They had laid a red carpet with flowers and balloons and our friends were there to greet us while a famous Arabic wedding song played and we made our way from the entrance to the splendid seats on stage.

As we sat on the kosha (the traditional Arabic chair that resembled a throne), we were overwhelmed with everyone who came in great numbers to congratulate us. We felt like a royal couple. There were 15 parts of the event to get through, from jewellery presentation and wearing to Arabic poetry, dinner for 150 guests, cutting the cake, and a live Somali band. We opened the wedding with verses from the Quran and we had two MCs in Somali and English.

One of the highlights was the traditional Somali dance of 'Wave Your Flag'. Instead of waving a flag, I was waved instead! As soon as the song started, I was dragged out and was being waved in the air like a flag. I was in a state of total delirious-joyfulness although I couldn't see the expression on my new wife's face. I'm sure she thought I would sustain further physical disabilities when I fell flat on my spine during this moment of madness.

Another highlight was seeing all of my friends come to celebrate. We had twenty different nationalities represented including two of my best friends, Hamood and Ziad,who travelled from Bahrain and the UK. In typical Somalian tradition ("funerals are of a private matter, while weddings are public events"), we had 300 gatecrashers which added to the fun.

The only sad thing was that many of my family couldn't come because of visa limitations from Somalia. Celebrating yet another milestone without my parents had become a disappointing theme in my life that I was learning to accept.

Only God knows if our marriage could have taken place without that phone call, between my mum and my mum-in-law, during the uncertain time of the marriage proposal.

Chapter 20
Embracing My Mission and Vision

Two days after the wedding, Deeqa and I flew to Langkawi Island in, Malaysia, for our honeymoon. From there, I followed my quest for adventure travelling and we visited new destinations together.

Back home, as we started to plan for a secure future together, applying we felt we had no choice other than to approach the banks for financial assistance. We were reluctant to get into debt but as Muslims, we felt humiliated as well. We didn't feel comfortable to apply for finance from my existing conventional bank, so we approached a local Islamic bank in the UAE. It refused to open an account for me because of my disability.

It was claimed that my visual impairment meant I was incapable of conducting my financial affairs in a safe manner. It was insisted that I delegate a sighted person with a full power of attorney to conduct all my financial affairs on my behalf.

This was extremely insulting and I explored everything possible to prove to the bank that I had been capable of running my financial affairs for many years. But as I was desperate for the finance, I was coerced into signing the power of attorney over to my wife. It wasn't an issue of trusting my wife, I trust her with my life, but I felt degraded into a retarded creature. I was so angry that the bank couldn't provide me with reasonable adjustments so I could be in charge of my finances just like I have been all my life with other banks.

This horrible experience unleashed a fighting dragon in me. After I exhausted my options with the management of this bank's branch, I turned to the local media and aired my exclusion case. Within less than 24 hours, I received a call from a representative of the Central Bank apologizing to me. They said what I had experienced was totally unacceptable and a clear case of discrimination, sharing with me documents outlining federal law that clearly stipulates the protection for persons with disability and their right to full and equal financial participation.

On the same day, I received a call from this local bank, saying that it did not have mechanisms to accommodate my case. An excuse that was worse than the sin itself.

I was hurt and disappointed by this experience. The UAE has been my home for almost a decade and, until then, I always felt empowered as a person with a disability. But as horrible as this experience was, I am now grateful for it. It reminded me of the many exclusion practices around the world and reconnected me with my passion for standing up for the inclusion cause. It also served as a clear reminder that for 15 per cent of the world's population, fate is determined by people who do not represent them in any way. It means that people like me need to do more to fulfill the United Nation Conventional Rights of Persons with Disability's slogan "Nothing about us, without us". After all, nobody can feel my pain as much as I do.

I know it's naïve to expect a rosy life where there is full equity and inclusion. But once I accepted that, it makes my life worth living because I have decided to immerse myself in the triumphs and difficulties of my life mission. When setbacks happen to me, it gives me the ammunition to take the driving seat and try to make a difference rather than demanding equity and inclusion from the backseat. That's why I established my consultancy and advocacy platform, Inclusive Horizons. We, as a community of people with disabilities, need to fulfill our duties of advocacy so we can reap the rewarding right of equity and inclusion. The experience also made me understand that although the goal of all disabled people around the world is the same (inclusion), the ways of achieving that goal must be relevant and sensitive at the local level.

Before I started my advocacy platform, I was with my first employer, MBC. Just after five years of working with them, I found I was unable to fulfill my ambitions there although I did my best with everything that was assigned to me. I put my case forward to initiate and carry out different programs, but I felt there was a lack of trust in my ability from my line managers to go the next level up. I wasn't comfortable with turning up every day just to keep doing the same again and again.

I started to satisfy my passion for making an impact by volunteering with the Emirates National Bank of Dubai as an advisor for their Corporate Social Responsibilities initiatives. It was my job to encourage more people with a disability to join. In addition, I improved my public-speaking skills, event management organization, content creation, and community outreach by helping to establish a professional network for Somali people. It was a chance to reconnect with my own community, to shift the mindset of our youth to believe in themselves and invest in their potential. I gained such pleasure in working closely with Abu-Baker (the founder of the network) which started with a few members in a small park to become the largest Somali network in the world connecting over 25,000 professionals, students, and entrepreneurs around five continents within five years.

In May 2017, though, I was made redundant from MBC. When the HR manager called me to the redundancy meeting, I remember they were surprised at how calmly I took the news. The truth was, I felt that a huge burden had been taken off of my shoulders.

I have so much appreciation for MBC for providing me with five years of employment, and all of the reasonable adjustments from which I benefited. I have plenty of wonderful memories. Ironically, from a personal point of view, the job loss was perfect timing as we were expecting our first baby. However, it was a disaster from a financial point of view as I was in debt with two separate banks. And I was now about to be the breadwinner for an extra person, as well as my responsibilities to the family back in Somalia.

Thank God, I was already in regular contact with Emirates National Bank of Dubai to convert my volunteering efforts into a full-time opportunity. There were several people who believed in my potential, and in particular, Maryam Bahlouq, who to see in me something that I didn't see myself. She asked if I'd thought about being a trainer who inspires people with my stories and style of delivery. She is one of those people that I call a foresighted leader.

I observed the perfection of God's plan for me. Just as I was let go from MBC, Maryam became the CEO of Tanfeeth—a subsidiary of the bank. After a few rounds of interviews, I managed to convince the hiring team to employ me in a creative function and after a few weeks, a suitable opportunity became vacant as Assistant Learning and Development Manager. I couldn't have wished for a better and more inclusive employer.

Before starting work, I felt a sudden intuition to travel alone. You might think this was somewhat selfish as my wife was nearing the delivery of our daughter. But I couldn't help it. I needed to connect with the green of nature, something I always seek when I am under pressure. I went to Kirgizstan and found it incredibly hospitable. Mountainous, lush, with elegant horses and beautiful lakes, it was simply magnificent. I climbed mountains and immersed myself in therapeutic waterfalls despite the fact I couldn't speak a word of Russian or local dialects. Frankly, this is what made my experience more adventurous. More than anything else, for the first time, people weren't fascinated by the fact that I am blind but because I am black. They were queuing up to take pictures with me! I found it amusing what people of different cultures are intrigued by.

I returned totally refreshed with plenty of energy to resume my new life as a father: my time in Kirgizstan allowed me to reset my priorities.

But before I tell you about the birth of my children, I have the hardest bit of the book to write. I cannot think of my daughters without a constant memory of my mother. You see, she had passed away peacefully in the same month, as my first daughter's due date, a year earlier, in 2016.

I was in the UK on an international assignment with Dialogue Social Enterprise running a series of workshops. On the third day, I woke up at 6.25 am; it was Wednesday, 24 August, and I was up and ready to join the team to go to the venue. When I got to the breakfast area, no one was there. What had happened to those punctual Germans? I ate my breakfast slowly, alone. An hour passed and just as I was about to give up, I saw all my colleagues. I had woken up an hour too early. I waited for them and we all headed out to the workshops.

When I returned in the evening and turned on my phone, I saw countless missed calls from my siblings: when I finally got in touch they told me that my mum had passed away. It had been at 8.25 am Somalia time, which is 6. 25am British time.

Coincidence? Of course not. I know there is a perfectionist who orchestrates everything and every matter in this universe. The fact I woke up at the exact time Mum died revealed a divine connection with my most beloved human on the Earth: despite our harsh separation of many years and thousands of miles.

Her death left me devastated especially as I couldn't go home for the funeral. Over the next few days, I thought about her relentless will to care and provide. My heart became filled with pride and admiration for her pure intention and while I knew her physical life was over, I prayed and promised that her legacy will live for as long as possible. Writing this book is hopefully the start of launching humanitarian initiatives in her memory.

It wasn't a coincidence either, then, that almost exactly a year later, Deeqa went into hospital to have our first baby. Maryam was born on 10 August 2017, at

2.36 pm, at City Hospital in Dubai, and the birth of our first daughter will remain forever in my heart. As Deeqa was wheeled into surgery, to have her Caesarean, I held her hand, terribly nervous but excited as well. There was a large plastic sheet covering Deeqa's body but I could see the moment when Maryam came out; suddenly I heard the cry and saw a beautiful, tiny thing up in the air. It sent me into another world. I *thought*, Really? Is she mine? Where did she come from?

I rushed forward to hold her, I couldn't wait for the nurses to wash the baby! They gave her to me as soon as they could, just barely minutes old. I remember they took her footprint and I held her and hugged her. It was an incredibly amazing and powerful moment to hold my own daughter. Before that day, I had never held a baby. I was worried I would drop someone else's child. Before the birth, I was concerned I wouldn't be able to hold our own baby. But my fears didn't eventuate. The intensity of happiness meant there was no space for worry.

I experienced overwhelming gratitude towards God for giving me a gift of my own child and, at the same time, I was fascinated by the science and surrealness of it all. How can two creatures have intercourse and that joyful moment translate into another human? How did this tiny girl survive in her mum's belly for nine months? How did she grow into this miniature human? I wondered what was going on in her head. Was she shocked after the birth? How can she be breathing for herself?

None of these questions had ever occurred to me before: I was holding someone as fresh as you can get!

I had a very strong sense of leadership at that moment. I realized for the rest of my life that I was responsible for a human being. I knew it; I had to raise my daughter in the best possible way and whatever she did in her life would be a reflection of me in some way, bad or good. I felt a sense of legacy and the need to step up to the challenge: I would no longer be just doing my own thing. I had a greater obligation towards Deeqa. I saw Deeqa, for the first time, as a mother and not as a wife. It was a very special and bonding moment. It was no longer a relationship between just the two of us, she was the mother of our child. I felt real and genuine respect toward her. I admired her calmness as she lay there with her stomach cut open.

The day my daughter was born had a greater significance. She became someone who would replace the intensity of losing my mum. Maryam's birth felt just as unreal and incredible as the day I met my mum after 22 years of separation. I hadn't been part of a family for so long because we lived continents apart. But that made it all the more special now, having a family of my own.

Less than three years later, our second daughter, Reem, was born on 17 March 2020, at 8.35 am, in the same hospital, by the same doctor.. Deeqa and I were both very grateful to His Mighty for having two beautiful children especially as my wife had endured many struggles to fall pregnant. I'd like to take a moment to admire and appreciate the struggle and sacrifice of our women and, in particular, our mothers. As a friend put it more light-heartedly: women have to put up with nine months of pregnancy and the pain of giving birth. What do men contribute? Three minutes of fun!

Reem's arrival made us complete. But she was born during the beginning of COVID-19 and it was a different experience. I didn't feel quite the same intense feelings as I had with Maryam. I still felt that wonderful connection and the joy of fatherhood when she arrived but we couldn't have visitors and I think this affected her personality. Reem is very shy and cries often. She isn't as confident as Maryam.

Raising children is hard for me. I've realized that now. Not because of my disability but because I'm not the most patient person. Some people are very family-orientated and would be happy to spend all their day with their children. I can't. I get bored quickly. As a young man, I grew up independent because I lived away from my family, that's just part of who I am. I am always on the go and love the feeling of being able to move countries any time; the thrill of taking on a crazy new job.

The way I looked after my family in Somalia was from a distance, as a provider by sharing my income. The way I show love to my children is to provide for them and work as hard for them as I can rather than feeding them and changing their nappies. What I most enjoy are our family holidays together: those intense, quality moments when we are all together.

As a young father, I began my new job with Tanfeeth in October 2017. I was welcomed and embraced warmly by everyone in the company. They offered me the most important thing that an organization can extend to someone with a disability the gift of trust. I asked for that during the interview and I certainly received it.

I was the Induction and Orientation program trainer for new joiners, as well as creating and delivering a wide range of soft skills and leadership training. The biggest impact I feel I made on that organization is creating a strong culture of coaching and development: I had all the support possible to create holistic coaching and a mentoring program for more than 100 managers and team leaders. It was made possible because of many development initiatives including the training investment that allowed me to become a certified Co-Active Professional Coach.

Generally, I was trusted to unleash my creativity and passion to initiate new programs and improve the process of existing ones. I was also empowered to contribute toward all the Diversity and Inclusion initiatives. All in all, it was a rewarding three years at a brilliant company that believed in and trusted in me even during the beginning of the COVID-19 pandemic.

Unfortunately, just like any journey, it came to an end and I made the tough decision to resign from Tanfeeth due to family reasons. I will always cherish the wonderful memories I made there and feel proud of what I achieved but mostly I feel gratitude for Tanfeeth's trust and support. While there are many people worthy of special mention, I want to share my appreciation for my immediate managers, Partika, Syed, Jowan and Fatima Abdulrahman, who were responsible for the catalyst of this gift of trust, as well as all my colleagues who supported me and shared meaningful interactions with me.

With a heavy heart, I share with you the loss of my dad on 19 December 2021 after years of battling with ill health. He was in poor general health and had had high blood pressure, with fluid on the stomach that had to be constantly removed. He passed away peacefully, at home, in Somalia with most of our family members with him, at the end. Just before that, he had booked a health trip to India but never got to go as he became severely ill.

I was in Bahrain at the time he passed away, in the middle of a coaching session that I was conducting. My phone kept ringing non-stop and I battled with the urge of answering it to hear what I have long feared. But I had to maintain my professionalism and compose myself as a coach. But after the session, I called my siblings back and heard the worst. I felt guilty about our missed opportunities and not being able to attend his funeral. It is difficult to comprehend not having either parent left in this world and not being able to go to your parents' funerals is a very strange feeling.

There was no strong emotional connection between my dad and me because of our physical separation: it was not normal to be so far apart with the additional language barrier, and not being able to share those day-to-day interactions and moments. But I loved him dearly because he had done so much for me from far away: it was a weird feeling. He managed to give me what I needed as a son by advising me as an adult and disciplining me as a child. I remember him telling me when I was very little: "God gave you two ears and one mouth, so make sure you listen more than you talk. That way you will get far in life by observing and being curious". His other physiological analogy often comes back to me: "If you look upwards and downwards, your neck hurts. In life, you should look ahead and focus on what you can influence rather than being influenced by those who are at a different level than yourself."

Only now because of losing both my parents who lived so far away do I find myself more connected with my two daughters. I focus on the joyful moments of raising kids: "Oh Baba, I will be your parent now," said my four-year-old daughter when she saw me upset one day and I told her my father had gone. It's priceless. Being a present father is a decision I've made: I'm accustomed to being away from people—I could go somewhere for a better job, a better prospect—but after I've thought about it, I realize there is nothing that could be worth it to miss my kids growing up. I was separated from my family because of war, and I must count my blessings. That's why I trust God. I don't know what is good for me. As painful as it was to be separated from my parents, it made me a lot more useful to my family. I am pleased with what God has planned for me. It doesn't matter how much you are dissatisfied, it won't change. The best way for things to improve is to accept it. Disability, poverty, illness: the moment you accept it, then you will get the best of the situation.

I believe a lot of us are in denial of our problems and as a result of that, people won't get out of it and it's a vicious circle of suffering. I'm not accepting it because I'm passive, I'm accepting it because it's God's justice. That's what gives me comfort. I cannot know everything but I do trust that someone else does. Be content. Be as ambitious as you can but be content. Otherwise, it will never be enough. When I am content, I find more comes my way.

While I'm here, I will always do what I can to make the most of my life and honour my mother and father.

Chapter 21

Connecting the Dots

After my current career break (God willing) that allowed me to write this book and have more time to connect with my family, I look forward to engaging in a fulfilling and exciting initiative either as an employee or self-employed. My next plan is to embark on a consultancy job and to research accessible technology. Whatever the future holds for me, I wish to pursue my mission toward a more inclusive and empowering world, and I particularly want to improve accessibility for people with a disability. I also want to build inspiring personal and professional life mindsets through my coaching and training. I hope each reader takes away something from this book because it wasn't my intention to share my story for the sake of it. I aim to illustrate my values, honour the endeavours of my mother, and shed light on different aspects of life from the point of view of a diverse individual who happens to be blind.

To sum up, below is an overview of some of the lessons I have learned. I hope they will be useful for you, either at an individual or organizational level:

1. Firstly, take care of your intention and God will take care of the outcome. My mum's intention to send me abroad was not to make us both endure hardship, but out of pure intention and strong will to build a brighter future for me. God's will took care of the details of this separation, and the wisdom and the outcome were far more rewarding than she ever wished for.

2. The notions of risk and trust are actually a complementary relationship rather than an adversarial one. Every thought and action in life has an element of both combined. Neither exists without the other.

3. The ability to forgive is the best gift you can give to yourself. I learned not to hold grudges against anyone (including those people who tortured me as a kid in Al-Noor school in Bahrain). One of the best lessons I learned about this subject, and I have coached several clients about it, was wisdom that I heard in a podcast called *Life is a Marathon*. As Bruce Van Horn says, "Forgiving someone purifies yourself from the poison of grudges: it does not mean letting free the person who did wrong to you. In other words, the notion

of justice has no bearing on your ability to move on for the sake of your own wellbeing." This idea is in line with my religion, which is my main source of my personal morality. The ability to let go had made space in my heart, mind, and spirit to be filled with hope, resilience, and determination.

4. If there is one relationship in life that's worth blood, sweat, and tears to maintain, it is the relationship with parents. You might have 99 reasons for cutting your parents off but I urge you to look for one reason to uphold this relationship.

5. Do not limit your contribution to society through your career's progression. Personally, I'd get rid of the word, career, altogether and replace it with something like a "productivity-mission" to better represent the multifaceted components of your current capabilities and potential that are beyond your 'job label', and are driven by a purpose, impact, and legacy. Your career is limited to less than one-third of your contribution, but the reality is that you will gain knowledge and skills from the moment you are born to the moment of death. No CV can capture life experience.

6. Do not let people's mental limitations determine your own potential. When people doubt or patronize you, they are in essence unwittingly projecting to you their own limitations, not yours. I learned this lesson in defiance of my doubters and also during the COVID-19 pandemic when my three-year-old

daughter proved me wrong and showed me how she could study online, at home.

7. Your pride to embrace your diversity must not mask your authenticity. Your different strands of diversity must complement the values of what makes you authentically unique. Further, someone's right to express their values must not be construed as intolerance towards others, just because of the difference in values. For example, I have no issue with certain people's reluctance not to embrace some strands of my diversity and I have the same right as long as we do not discriminate between one another. Beyond the obvious strands of diversity, I feel the true value of diversity can be realized through the diversity of thought, where the focus is on ideas and approaches. For example, my friend, Ali Duallah: despite our identical backgrounds, often he is the one who provides me with the most diverse, contrasting, and pragmatic ideas. When it comes to inclusion, I believe that all levels of inclusion from the individual to the policy level can be strengthened by learning through a crisis. Major incidents serve to challenge our assumptions and change the status quo.

8. Independence, accessibility, reasonable adjustments, and trust are the most effective tools to empower people living with a disability. Accessibility provisions are not only helpful to the 15% of the world's population who live with a permanent disability, but useful to

millions of other people who experience a temporary and situational form of disability. Relevant accessibility provisions are the most effective tool to break the intertwined chain of disability and poverty. While I am not an expert in Inclusive Education, I believe from my own experience that the educational integration of people with disabilities in mainstream schools is best if it starts from the age of 15. This blended approach, for early special education, and then, integration into mainstream education, allows for the healthiest development and inclusion. Disabled people want reasonable adjustments and empathy; not privileges or sympathy. Regardless of the type of our disability, we do not feel that we are sick and need to be cured. Neither do we want people to be afraid to ask about disability and break taboos. We see ourselves as another fabric of any society, one that is capable of contributing positively.

9. Justice and equity is an admirable goal, but we are all going to view it differently. This goal is something that particularly can be progressed toward through the application of struggle and pursuit rather than the virtue of expectation. This is for many reasons, but in particular because of the fact that every step forward for justice and equity will inevitably mean the compromise for someone else's privilege. Every small step we take towards this goal has a much bigger impact than we realize, especially through the power of mass-media.

10. Perseverance must revolve around the notion of contentment. We all are required to persevere as hard as we can to pursue excellence. This spirit ironically reminds me of a wise saying that I read in a book written by a blind woman called *Blind Ambitions*. She says: "Every morning we wake up with two choices, either we roll back to bed and continue to dream our dreams, or we get up and live our dreams." This emphasizes the importance of sparing no energy in the pursuits of our passions. And I'll add that we must never lose gratitude for our blessings, in the process. Persevering does not mean stubbornness, but instead clarity of vision and the ability to be intuitive enough to change course as necessary. To me, contentment is the perfect psychological state as it allows you to be grounded and embrace life to the fullest irrespective of the heights of triumphs or the lows of tribulations.

The story of triumphs and tribulations of the unshakeable will in the search for inclusion and equity is throughout this book. However, there is a much I stronger unshakeable will that underpinned my story. Remember my invitation to you at the start of this book to learn from the experiences in this life and keep expanding? As a passionate learner and student of life, I always have been fascinated by the art of self-learning. I am here talking about active learning as supposed to passive learning.

Every blessing or a tough or a joyful moment from the moment when I was an embryo until today could not have been operating by random intricacies. Every discipline that I have studied since grade 1, until my latest educational attainment, are all guiding me to the same path of the One who is guiding my journey, and everyone's journey, should they wish to tap into that strength. On a personal level, and as you have been reading so far, I had no present parents to learn from yet, despite everything I have gone through, I always had a Merciful and Compassionate eye that looks after me and wisdom that enlightens me. This divine connection is what gifted me with the art of reflection and allowed me to learn through a receptive yet critical lens. While I do not want to claim that I have lived like an angel, as I have made many mistakes and committed countless errors, never have I lost my connection with The Divine.

My own conclusion when reflecting and pondering profoundly on this flawless universe, is that there is a perfect God that has created it and chosen us exclusively to be here. This God or higher power is beyond human imagination and beyond any representation. It is beyond space and time, race, and gender. Given the perfection of the universe in its entirety, it is only possible to me that this God is absolute, in every sense of the word. For me to reach this outcome, I had first *not* to follow blindly the values I grew up with but instead be as objective as possible with my five senses. This quest has propelled me to look within myself, my surroundings, and everything in the horizons of this universe. I have shared my thoughts explicitly as a Muslim in this book as I learned the importance of living an authentic life. After all, I'd be anything but authentic if I feel something and say something else, just to gain people's approval.

After so many years of bewilderment and identity crises, the gift of intention, intuition, and reflection has allowed me to embrace my religion as the most meaningful identity that informs everything I say and do. I never chose my place of birth, my skin color, my disability, and certainly, I was not fully in charge of my social mobility and opportunities in life. However, through the power of choice, I understand that my religion is the campus that can shed the light on anything. To me, Islam is the only guidance that helped me to understand my life, from appropriate behaviors of bedroom intimacy to under-standing the most complex geological and astrology phenomena. This powerful inclusivity is what makes my religion worthy of representing and governing the multi-faceted aspects of my diverse identity. To me, separating religion from society is like removing a soul from the body: the body will become rotten without its living soul.

Everything discussed in this book is a modest attempt to share with you the power of one human's will. This unshakeable will empowers us all as humans to fulfill all our missions on this earth. All of what I have shared is purely from my point of view as an avid seeker of knowledge. You have the capability to pick and choose your takeaways and further ponder on any themes relevant to you. I once again, thank you sincerely for your choice to read some of my thoughts. I'll be delighted to engage with you through different platforms to inspire one another.